SITTING ASIDE

THE ART AND SCIENCE OF SUCCESSION PLANNING

SIDHISHWARR N RINDHE

This book is dedicated to all those who embody the spirit of acceptance, respect, and love. Your commitment to embracing diversity and fostering inclusivity creates a foundation for positive change in our communities and organizations.

May this dedication serve as a tribute to individuals and organizations working tirelessly towards sustainability through the lens of succession planning. Your efforts in nurturing the next generation of leaders contribute to a brighter, more harmonious future for us all.

With gratitude for your unwavering dedication and involvment.

Contents

Preface

In the vast tapestry of epic tales, where heroes rise and kingdoms fall, the profound lessons of succession planning echo through the corridors of time. "Sitting Aside" embarks on a journey to unravel the importance and intricate strategies entwined in the art of succession planning, drawing inspiration from the timeless narratives of the Ramayana and Mahabharata.

As we navigate the complexities of leadership transitions, we find ourselves at the crossroads of ancient wisdom and contemporary challenges. The narratives of Lord Rama, Krishna, Yudhishthira, and others become beacons guiding us through the nuances of strategic decision-making, visionary leadership, mentorship, and effective communication – the pillars upon which successful successions are built. In the pages that follow, we delve into the consequences of neglecting succession through the lens of Dhritarashtra's blindness, explore visionary leadership exemplified by Lord Rama, and unravel the delicate dance of family dynamics as seen in the challenges faced by Sita and Kaikeyi. Each chapter unveils valuable insights, offering a blueprint for crafting successful succession narratives. The lessons from the Mahabharata's Kauravas dilemma become a cautionary tale, illustrating the impact of flawed decisions on the succession of Hastinapura. Yudhishthira's leadership qualities guide us through the storms of adversity, while Krishna's wisdom serves as a metaphor for mentorship, providing a roadmap for leaders to guide their successors with sagacity.

Bhishma Pitamah's communication strategies offer a masterclass in conveying crucial succession-related information, and Ravana's downfall becomes a stark reminder of the consequences of lacking a structured succession plan. The exemplary rule of Bharata beckons us to investigate the commitment to upholding family legacy, and the Pandavas in exile become a source of inspiration for navigating change and embracing adaptability. The insights drawn from the dice game in the Mahabharata unveil a case study for handling conflicts within a family during succession, shedding light on effective conflict resolution strategies. Each narrative serves as a living testament to the enduring principles that underpin the fabric of successful leadership transitions.

As we embark on this exploration, let "Sitting Aside" be your companion, weaving together ancient sagas and contemporary paradigms to illuminate the path toward crafting your succession epic. May these pages inspire leaders, aspiring and seasoned alike, to embrace the wisdom of the past, charting a course for success in the ever-evolving landscape of leadership transitions.
-Sidhishwarr

CHAPTER ONE

Introduction to Succession Planning

Succession planning, a strategic process essential for the longevity and prosperity of organizations, finds profound wisdom in the timeless epics of Mahabharata and Ramayana. These ancient narratives serve as rich repositories of invaluable lessons, offering unique insights into the consequences of neglecting or embracing succession planning.

The concept of succession planning revolves around ensuring a smooth transition of leadership within an organization. It is not merely a procedural formality but a dynamic strategy that shapes the future of an institution. Drawing inspiration from the Mahabharata and Ramayana, we can unravel the layers of significance embedded in this crucial organizational practice. In the Mahabharata, the narrative is woven around the succession dilemma in the Kuru dynasty. King Dhritarashtra's blindness, both metaphorical and literal, becomes a poignant symbol of the consequences of neglecting succession planning. His inability to address the rightful heir, fuelled by familial favouritism, leads to a catastrophic war – the Kurukshetra War.

The lesson here is clear – turning a blind eye to the intricacies of succession can have far-reaching consequences. Organizations too, when blind to the need for a well-defined succession plan, risk internal strife, power struggles, and a loss of strategic direction. It emphasizes the imperative for leaders to see beyond their immediate tenure and strategically plan for a seamless transition. In contrast, the Ramayana presents an exemplary model of visionary leadership through Lord Rama. His principled and visionary approach serves as a guiding light for succession planning in organizations. Rama's commitment to dharma (righteousness) and his unwavering focus on the greater good set the stage for an ideal succession scenario.

Rama's exile, a pivotal moment in the Ramayana, is akin to a leader's transitional phase. Despite facing adversity, Rama's commitment to his principles remains unshaken. This illustrates that succession planning isn't about choosing a successor but instilling a set of values and principles that will endure beyond the current leadership.

The Mahabharata and Ramayana underscore the importance of identifying and nurturing leadership qualities, exemplified by characters like Yudhishthira and Lord Rama. Yudhishthira's leadership during the challenges of the dice game and exile showcases qualities such as resilience, strategic thinking, and the ability to navigate adversity – all essential traits for a leader steering an organization through transitions. Krishna's role as a mentor to Arjuna in the Mahabharata echoes the significance of mentorship in succession planning. Arjuna's initial hesitation and confusion represent the uncertainties that successors may face. Krishna's guidance not only provides clarity but also emphasizes the role of experienced mentors in shaping the future leaders of an organization.

Navigating family dynamics, as seen in the challenges faced by Sita and Kaikeyi, becomes a pertinent analogy for organizations dealing with internal power structures and familial influences. Organizations must acknowledge and address familial complexities to ensure a smooth transition of leadership without succumbing to internal strife. Effective communication, a cornerstone of successful succession planning, is exemplified by Bhishma Pitamah in the Mahabharata. His communication strategies, especially during the Kurukshetra War, highlight the importance of transparent and timely communication in times of organizational transition.

Building a robust succession framework, as showcased by Bharata's exemplary rule in the Ramayana, emphasizes the need for a structured and well-thought-out plan. Bharata's commitment to upholding the family legacy becomes a beacon for organizations seeking continuity and stability in leadership transitions.

The adaptability and change management skills displayed by the Pandavas during their exile offer valuable lessons for organizations operating in dynamic environments. The Pandavas' ability to adapt and navigate challenges underscores the importance of agility in succession planning.

Conflict resolution, exemplified by the lessons from the dice game in the Mahabharata, becomes a critical aspect of succession planning.

Organizations must learn from the conflicts within the family to develop strategies for handling internal disputes during leadership transitions.

Examining leadership transitions, such as Sugriva's success in the Ramayana, provides insights into the importance of a smooth handover of responsibilities. Sugriva's transition illustrates the positive outcomes of a well-managed leadership change, ensuring continuity and stability.

Inclusive leadership, influenced by Draupadi's role in the Mahabharata, highlights the significance of diversity and inclusivity in leadership teams. Organizations must recognize the impact of inclusive leadership on fostering a positive and collaborative work culture during succession.

Managing opposition, as seen in Vibhishana's loyalty shift in the Ramayana, sheds light on the challenges of dealing with dissent during succession. Understanding and effectively managing opposition is crucial for maintaining organizational cohesion.

Ethical decision-making, exemplified by Lord Rama's adherence to principles during exile, emphasizes the importance of ethical conduct in leadership transitions. Organizations must prioritize ethics to ensure a seamless and morally sound succession process.

Balancing tradition and innovation, as demonstrated by Hanuman's wisdom in the Ramayana, becomes a guiding principle for organizations navigating the delicate balance between preserving traditions and embracing innovation during succession planning.

In conclusion, the insights gleaned from the Mahabharata and Ramayana offer a comprehensive guide to the intricacies of succession planning. By weaving these timeless lessons into the fabric of organizational strategies, leaders can craft their own success epics, ensuring a legacy that endures beyond their tenure. The path to strategic success lies not just in choosing the right successor but in embracing a holistic approach that encompasses values, mentorship, communication, and adaptability – all crucial elements drawn from the sagas of Mahabharata and Ramayana.

CHAPTER TWO

The Blind Spot: Lessons from Dhritarashtra

Dhritarashtra's Legacy of Neglect in Succession Planning

In the intricate tapestry of the Mahabharata, one character's blindness serves as a powerful metaphor for the dire consequences of neglecting succession planning. Dhritarashtra, the blind king of Hastinapura, becomes emblematic of the blind spots that can plague leadership, particularly when it comes to the critical aspect of succession. In this exploration, we delve into the lessons embedded in Dhritarashtra's story, unravelling the repercussions of his failure to avert the catastrophic Kurukshetra War. As we navigate this ancient narrative, we draw parallels to contemporary organizational challenges, urging leaders to address their own blind spots and fortify their succession strategies.

The Blind King's Tragedy

Dhritarashtra's tale is one of tragedy woven with missed opportunities and a failure to address the succession question. His literal blindness becomes symbolic of the figurative blindness that leaders can develop when they overlook the imperative of planning for the future. As the blind monarch of Hastinapura, Dhritarashtra was entrusted with the responsibility of securing a prosperous future for his kingdom, yet his inability to see beyond his immediate concerns paved the way for a destructive war.

Leadership Blind Spots in Succession

Dhritarashtra's blind spot was not just a physical ailment but a manifestation of a broader leadership blind spot – the inability to foresee and navigate the challenges of succession. In the organizational realm, this serves as a cautionary tale for leaders who might be turning a blind eye to the impending need for a well-thought-out succession plan. The consequences of such oversight can be as devastating as the war that unfolded in the Mahabharata.

Lessons for Modern Leaders

As we dissect Dhritarashtra's missteps, the lessons for modern leaders become starkly apparent. Neglecting succession planning can lead to internal strife, power struggles, and a loss of strategic direction. The blind spot extends beyond the immediate leader to impact the very fabric of the organization, much like the ripples of discord that emanated from Dhritarashtra's lack of foresight.

Parallel Challenges in Modern Organizations

Drawing parallels to contemporary organizational challenges, we witness instances where leaders, consumed by the urgencies of the present, inadvertently neglect the imperatives of the future. The blind spot persists in boardrooms and executive offices, with leaders failing to recognize the significance of grooming and preparing the next generation of leadership. The consequences may not be as stark as a war, but they can lead to a gradual erosion of organizational resilience and competitiveness.

Addressing the Blind Spot

Avert the tragedy of a leadership blind spot, it is imperative for modern leaders to confront the looming challenges of succession planning head-on. Dhritarashtra's story serves as a call to action, urging leaders to recognize the limitations of their vision and proactively address the succession question.

Foresight and Vision: The Antidote to Blindness

Dhritarashtra's story underscores the importance of developing foresight and vision in leadership. Modern leaders must cultivate the ability to see beyond the immediate horizon, anticipating the changes and challenges that lie ahead. By adopting an initiative-taking stance, leaders can navigate the complexities of succession with clarity and purpose.

Transparency in Leadership: Removing the Veil of Ignorance

Dhritarashtra's reluctance to confront the reality of his son Duryodhana's actions is a poignant lesson in the perils of leadership opacity. Modern organizations should prioritize transparency in leadership, fostering open communication about succession plans and ensuring that key stakeholders are aware of the strategic direction.

Inclusive Decision-Making: Breaking Free from Isolation

The isolation Dhritarashtra maintained in making critical decisions for his kingdom serves as a stark warning against leadership seclusion. Modern leaders must embrace inclusive decision-making processes, involving key stakeholders in succession discussions to ensure a comprehensive and well-considered strategy.

Empowering the Next Generation: Breaking the Chains of Dependency

Dhritarashtra's overreliance on his son Duryodhana resulted in a skewed succession path, marked by nepotism and favouritism. Modern organizations should focus on empowering a diverse pool of talent, breaking free from dependency on a single individual and ensuring a merit-based approach to succession.

Building a Succession Culture: Sowing Seeds for the Future

Dhritarashtra's failure to establish a culture of succession planning highlights the need for modern leaders to embed this practice into the organizational DNA. Building a succession culture involves consistently identifying and nurturing potential leaders, creating a pipeline that ensures a seamless transition when the time comes.

Risk Mitigation Strategies: Preventing the Kurukshetra Within

The Kurukshetra War, born out of Dhritarashtra's negligence, serves as a stark reminder of the risks associated with leadership blind spots. Modern leaders must develop robust risk mitigation strategies, anticipating potential conflicts and challenges that may arise during succession transitions.

Learning from Mistakes: Embracing Continuous Improvement

Dhritarashtra's tragic tale is not without its share of mistakes. Modern leaders should adopt a mindset of continuous improvement, learning from historical missteps and refining succession strategies based on evolving organizational needs.

As we unravel the blind spot in Dhritarashtra's story, the resonance with modern leadership challenges becomes undeniable. The consequences of neglecting succession planning, evident in the Kurukshetra War, serve as a cautionary tale for leaders navigating the complexities of organizational dynamics. The call to action is clear – modern leaders must confront their blind spots, cultivate foresight, and actively engage in shaping a robust succession strategy. By learning from the ancient echoes of the Mahabharata, leaders can ensure that their legacy is one of strategic foresight, organizational resilience, and enduring success.

Nokia's Blindness to Smartphone Transition:

In the early 2000s, Nokia was a global leader in mobile phones, much like Dhritarashtra's reign over Hastinapura. However, Nokia failed to recognize the impending shift to smartphones. The company's leadership was blind to the changing landscape of mobile technology, neglecting the importance of a successful succession strategy. Consequently, Nokia lost its dominant position in the market, reminiscent of Hastinapura's downfall due to Dhritarashtra's negligence.

Blockbuster's Oversight of Digital Streaming:

Blockbuster, once a giant in the video rental industry, failed to foresee the rise of digital streaming platforms. Similar to Dhritarashtra's inability to address the rightful heir, Blockbuster neglected to adapt to the changing preferences of consumers. This blind spot in succession planning led to the company's decline, as competitors embraced the digital age, leaving Blockbuster in the shadows of its past glory.

Kodak's Inability to Embrace Digital Photography:

Kodak, a pioneer in the photography industry, faced a similar blind spot as Dhritarashtra when it came to the digital revolution. Despite being a powerhouse in film photography, Kodak neglected the potential of digital imaging. The company's failure to adapt and groom a successor technology led to its decline, emphasizing the importance of addressing the blind spots in succession planning.

Yahoo's Leadership Changes and Missed Opportunities:

Yahoo, once a dominant player in the tech industry, struggled with leadership changes and missed opportunities. Dhritarashtra's neglect of rightful succession finds parallels in Yahoo's frequent leadership changes and failure to harness emerging trends. This blind spot hindered Yahoo's ability to compete effectively, eventually leading to its diminished relevance in the tech landscape.

Sears' Decline Amid E-commerce Rise:

Sears, a retail giant for over a century, faced a blind spot akin to Dhritarashtra's neglect of succession. As e-commerce emerged, Sears failed to adapt its business model, reminiscent of the blind king's failure to address the rightful heir. The company's decline underscores the repercussions of overlooking critical succession planning, leaving it unprepared for the evolving retail landscape.

Dhritarashtra's blind spot in neglecting succession planning serves as a stark reminder for contemporary organizations. The consequences of failing to groom competent successors, adapt to changing landscapes, and address internal challenges can be dire. The examples of Nokia, Blockbuster, Kodak, Yahoo, and Sears illustrate that organizations, like kingdoms, must be vigilant and strategic in succession planning to avoid falling victim to their blind spots. By learning from these cautionary tales, businesses can chart a course that ensures long-term success and resilience in the face of evolving landscapes.

CHAPTER THREE

Visionary Leadership: Lord Rama's Legacy

Unveiling Rama's Vision: A Blueprint for Visionary Leadership in Succession Planning

In the grand tapestry of epic tales, none shines as brightly as the Ramayana, and at its heart lies the archetype of a visionary leader – Lord Rama. This exploration delves into the essence of Rama's principled leadership, extracting timeless lessons that transcend the ages and echo in the corridors of contemporary leadership. As we journey through the chapters of the Ramayana, we unravel the intricate threads that weave together Rama's legacy and its applicability as a potent model for cultivating a visionary approach in the realm of succession planning.

The Tapestry of Principled Leadership:

Lord Rama's story is not merely a myth but a reservoir of profound leadership wisdom. His principled leadership, rooted in dharma (righteousness), loyalty, and unwavering commitment, provides a compelling blueprint for leaders navigating the intricate landscape of succession planning. Rama's journey becomes a metaphorical map, guiding leaders to embrace a vision that extends beyond the immediate horizon.

Dharma as the Guiding Light: Crafting a Moral Compass

At the core of Rama's leadership is an unswerving commitment to dharma. His adherence to moral and ethical principles becomes the bedrock of his reign. In the realm of succession planning, this illuminates the path for leaders to craft a moral compass that steers decisions, ensuring that the legacy handed over is not just one of success but also of integrity.

The Vision Beyond the Self: Selflessness in Leadership

Rama's selfless dedication to the well-being of his subjects transcends personal desires. In the context of succession planning, this serves as a beacon for leaders to cultivate a selfless mindset, placing the organization's long-term prosperity above individual ambitions. A visionary leader looks beyond personal gains, focusing on the enduring success of the collective.

Integrity in Decision-Making: Navigating the Moral Crossroads

Rama's unwavering integrity in decision-making, even when faced with formidable challenges, becomes a hallmark of his leadership. Leaders engaged in succession planning can draw inspiration to navigate the moral crossroads with integrity. Making decisions that align with ethical principles ensures a legacy untarnished by compromise.

Resilience in the Face of Adversity: Weathering the Storms

Rama's exile and subsequent challenges underscore the resilience inherent in visionary leadership. In the context of succession planning, leaders must anticipate and prepare for adversities. Resilience becomes the armour that shields the organization during transitional phases, ensuring continuity and stability despite the storms.

Strategic Patience: Nurturing Long-Term Objectives

Rama's strategic patience, evident in his wait for Sita and the meticulous planning for the war with Ravana, exemplifies the importance of nurturing long-term objectives. In succession planning, leaders are urged to adopt a patient and strategic mindset, understanding that the fruits of careful planning may take time to manifest.

Leading by Example: The Power of Exemplary Conduct

Rama's leadership is not dictatorial but one of leading by example. In the realm of succession planning, this becomes a call for leaders to embody the values they wish to perpetuate. A visionary leader's conduct becomes the benchmark for those who follow, setting the tone for a culture that endures beyond the current leadership.

Inclusive Governance: Fostering a Collaborative Approach

Rama's inclusive governance, seeking counsel from diverse voices and embracing Sugriva and Hanuman as integral allies, advocates for a collaborative approach. In succession planning, leaders are encouraged to embrace inclusivity, involving a diverse range of perspectives to formulate comprehensive strategies that resonate with the entire organizational ecosystem.

Commitment to Development: Nurturing the Next Generation

Rama's mentorship of Hanuman and the vanaras (monkeys) exemplifies a commitment to developing the next generation of leaders. In the realm of succession planning, this serves as a reminder for leaders to actively engage in mentoring and nurturing talent, ensuring a smooth transition and the continuous growth of leadership capabilities.

Strategic Communication: Crafting a Narrative of Unity

Rama's communication, both with allies and adversaries, is marked by clarity and strategic precision. Leaders engaged in succession planning can glean insights into crafting a narrative that unifies rather than divides. Effective communication becomes the bridge that connects the past, present, and future, ensuring a seamless transition story.

Legacy Beyond Leadership: Building Enduring Foundations

Rama's legacy extends beyond his years of leadership. In the context of succession planning, leaders are urged to build enduring foundations that outlast their tenure. A visionary leader is not merely focused on short-term successes but lays the groundwork for sustained prosperity that resonates through generations.

As we traverse the landscape of Lord Rama's principled leadership in the Ramayana, the resonance with contemporary leadership challenges is unmistakable. The blueprint drawn from his legacy becomes a guidebook for leaders navigating the complexities of succession planning. Rama's story encapsulates the essence of visionary leadership – a leadership that transcends personal ambitions, navigates moral complexities with integrity, and fosters a legacy that extends far beyond the leader's time.

In the symphony of leadership, Rama's melody plays a timeless tune, inviting leaders to harmonize their approach to succession planning with the enduring notes of dharma, selflessness, resilience, and strategic vision. The legacy of Rama beckons leaders to not merely lead but to lead with purpose, leaving behind a trail of visionary footsteps for others to follow.

As we delve into Rama's legacy, we can draw parallels with contemporary organizations that exemplify visionary leadership, setting a benchmark for navigating successions with steadfast principles and forward-thinking strategies.

Elon Musk and Tesla's Visionary Trajectory:

Lord Rama's unwavering commitment to principles finds resonance in Elon Musk's visionary leadership at Tesla. Musk's steadfast dedication to sustainability, innovation, and technological advancement mirrors Rama's principled approach. Tesla's success in revolutionizing the automotive industry serves as a contemporary testament to the impact of visionary leadership on succession planning.

Satya Nadella's Microsoft Transformation:

Satya Nadella's tenure as the CEO of Microsoft aligns with Lord Rama's principled leadership in fostering a visionary approach. Rama prioritized dharma, and Nadella, in steering Microsoft, focused on values such as empathy, inclusivity, and continuous innovation. The company's successful transformation under Nadella's leadership reflects a visionary succession plan rooted in principled values.

Tim Cook and Apple's Evolution:

Lord Rama's legacy emphasizes the importance of visionary leaders who uphold principles even in the face of challenges. Tim Cook, as the CEO of Apple, has continued the legacy of innovation and customer-centric values established by Steve Jobs. Apple's sustained success in the post-Jobs era highlights the effectiveness of visionary leadership in ensuring a seamless succession.

Indra Nooyi's Impact at PepsiCo:

Indra Nooyi's tenure as the CEO of PepsiCo aligns with Lord Rama's principled leadership, emphasizing values and long-term vision. Rama's commitment to righteousness is reflected in Nooyi's focus on sustainability, corporate responsibility, and innovation. PepsiCo's ability to adapt to changing consumer preferences under Nooyi's leadership showcases the visionary principles embedded in succession planning.

Jeff Bezos and Amazon's Enduring Innovation:

Lord Rama's legacy underscores the importance of leaders who embrace innovation while adhering to principled values. Jeff Bezos, the founder of Amazon, exemplifies this visionary leadership by fostering a culture of continuous innovation and customer-centricity. Amazon's sustained growth and adaptability to market changes reflect the effectiveness of visionary succession planning under Bezos's principles.

Mark Benioff and Salesforce's Ethical Leadership:

Lord Rama's emphasis on ethical leadership finds resonance in Mark Benioff's visionary approach at Salesforce. Rama's commitment to dharma aligns with Benioff's focus on ethical business practices, social responsibility, and equality. Salesforce's success under Benioff's leadership illustrates the impact of principled vision on long-term succession planning.

Lord Rama's legacy serves as an enduring source of inspiration for cultivating visionary leadership in succession planning. Contemporary leaders like Elon Musk, Satya Nadella, Tim Cook, Indra Nooyi, Jeff Bezos, and Mark Benioff exemplify the principles of Rama's leadership in diverse organizational landscapes. By embracing principled vision, these leaders have not only ensured their organizations' continued success but have also set a standard for effective succession planning that aligns with enduring values and forward-thinking strategies.

• 13 •

CHAPTER FOUR

Strategic Decision-Making: The Kauravas Dilemma

Navigating the Battlefield of Decision-Making: Lessons from the Kauravas Dilemma in Succession

In the annals of epic sagas, none encapsulates the intricacies of decision-making quite like the Mahabharata, where the Kauravas' flawed choices become a cautionary tale echoing through the corridors of leadership. This exploration delves into the labyrinth of strategic decision-making, unravelling the Kauravas Dilemma and its far-reaching consequences on the succession of Hastinapura. As we embark on this journey through the pages of the Mahabharata, we unravel the threads of flawed decisions that, like a poisoned chalice, altered the destiny of a kingdom.

The Chessboard of Flawed Decisions:

The Kauravas, a symbol of ambition veering into the realm of hubris, found themselves ensnared in a web of misguided choices. The strategic blunders committed by Duryodhana, and his allies sowed the seeds of destruction, leading to the cataclysmic war at Kurukshetra. In the realm of succession, their story serves as a chilling reminder of the perils that befall leaders who disregard the importance of strategic decision-making.

Ambition vs. Prudence: The Lure of Unbridled Ambition

The Kauravas' blind pursuit of power and the throne is a stark reminder of the pitfalls of unbridled ambition. In the context of succession planning, leaders are urged to balance ambition with prudence, ensuring that strategic decisions are anchored in a clear understanding of the consequences.

The Poison of Ego: Duryodhana's Costly Pride

Duryodhana's unyielding pride becomes a tragic flaw that reverberates through the Mahabharata. In the arena of strategic decision-making, leaders are cautioned against the poison of unchecked ego. Decision-makers must rise above personal pride and ego-driven choices to secure the legacy of succession.

Consulting the Wise: The Importance of Sage Counsel

The Kauravas' reluctance to seek wise counsel, especially from Vidura and Bhishma, is a grave misstep. In the domain of succession planning, leaders are encouraged to humbly seek the counsel of experienced advisors. The wisdom of sage advice can illuminate the path through the complex chessboard of strategic decisions.

The Cost of Unjust Actions: Draupadi's Disrobing as a Symbol

The infamous episode of Draupadi's disrobing stands as a metaphor for the cost of unjust actions. In succession planning, leaders must be mindful of the repercussions of unethical decisions, as they can tarnish the reputation of the organization and erode the foundation upon which succession rests.

The Dice Game: A High-Stakes Gamble with Consequences

The ill-fated dice game, marked by deceit and manipulation, represents the perilous nature of high-stakes gambles. In the realm of succession, leaders are urged to approach strategic decisions with a clear understanding of the risks involved. A gamble gone awry can jeopardize not only the leader but the entire succession process.

Blind Spots in Leadership: The Role of Dhritarashtra

Dhritarashtra's blind indulgence in his son Duryodhana's desires symbolizes the blind spots that can plague leadership. In succession planning, leaders must actively identify and address these blind spots, ensuring that personal biases do not cloud the judgment needed for sound strategic decision-making.

The Consequences of Hubris: Duryodhana's Downfall

Duryodhana's overconfidence and disregard for righteous advice become the harbingers of his downfall. In the context of succession, leaders are reminded that hubris can lead to irreversible consequences. Humility and a willingness to reassess decisions are essential for long-term success.

Sibling Rivalry: The Impact on Unified Leadership

The Kauravas' internal strife, fuelled by sibling rivalry, fractured their potential for unified leadership. In succession planning, leaders are encouraged to foster unity among potential successors, ensuring that internal discord doesn't undermine the organization's stability during transitions.

Neglecting Moral Values: The Fall of Karna

Karna's fall due to his allegiance to Duryodhana, despite knowing the moral implications, underscores the importance of upholding ethical values. In succession planning, leaders must prioritize moral integrity, as the consequences of compromising ethical standards can reverberate through the organizational framework.

The Role of Karma: Weaving Destiny through Decisions

The concept of karma, intricately woven into the Mahabharata, teaches us that decisions shape destiny. In the realm of succession, leaders are reminded that each decision has a karmic imprint, influencing the organization's fate and the legacy left for future leaders.

As we unravel the saga of the Kauravas Dilemma, the echoes of flawed decisions reverberate through time, carrying profound implications for leaders charting the course of succession planning. The chessboard of strategic decision-making, painted with the hues of ambition, ego, and ethical choices, becomes a tapestry from which modern leaders can glean valuable insights.

The Kauravas' tragic narrative serves as a cautionary tale, urging leaders to tread carefully through the complex labyrinth of succession planning. Ambition, when tempered with prudence, ego checked by humility, and decisions guided by ethical considerations, paves the way for a legacy that withstands the tests of time. The lessons from the Kauravas Dilemma beckon leaders to navigate the chessboard of strategic decision-making with sagacity, ensuring that the succession journey is marked by wisdom, foresight, and a commitment to the enduring prosperity of the organization.

Nokia's Failure to Embrace Smartphones

Much like the Kauravas' flawed decisions that led to the devastation of Hastinapura, Nokia's failure to embrace smartphones serves as a modern-day illustration. The Kauravas' ambition and disregard for fairness in the game of dice parallel Nokia's overreliance on traditional mobile phones. Nokia's strategic decision to resist the shift to smartphones resulted in a significant loss of market share and exemplifies the consequences of flawed decision-making in the context of succession planning.

CHAPTER FIVE

Yudhishthira's Leadership Qualities

The Quintessence of Leadership: Unrávelling Yudhishthira's Traits for Seamless Transitions Amidst Adversity

In the labyrinth of ancient epics, the Mahabharata stands as an indomitable colossus, with Yudhishthira emerging as a beacon of leadership amidst the tumultuous tide of adversity. This exploration delves into the nuanced qualities that define Yudhishthira's leadership, serving as a guiding star for modern leaders navigating the turbulent waters of succession planning. As we embark on this odyssey through the pages of the Mahabharata, we unravel the tapestry of leadership traits that transforms adversity into an opportunity for seamless transition.

The Symphony of Leadership:

Yudhishthira, the eldest of the Pandavas, stands as a paragon of virtue and sagacity in the Mahabharata. His leadership journey is a symphony played in the face of challenges, showcasing an orchestra of qualities that resonate through time. As we dissect these qualities, we unearth invaluable lessons for leaders steering their organizations through the tempests of succession amidst adversity.

Dharma as the North Star: Guiding Leadership with Virtue

At the core of Yudhishthira's leadership is an unwavering commitment to dharma (righteousness). In the realm of succession planning, leaders are beckoned to anchor their decisions in the compass of virtue. Yudhishthira's adherence to dharma becomes the North Star, guiding leaders through the moral maze of transitions.

Calm Amidst the Storm: Yudhishthira's Unruffled Composure

Yudhishthira's poised composure, even in the face of calamity, is a testament to the power of calm leadership. In the realm of succession amidst adversity, leaders are encouraged to emulate his tranquillity. A steady hand at the helm ensures that transitions, though turbulent, are navigated with precision.

Inclusive Decision-Making: Weaving a Tapestry of Unity

Yudhishthira's approach to decision-making is inclusive, weaving a tapestry of unity among the Pandavas. In the context of succession planning, leaders are urged to foster a collaborative environment. Inclusivity becomes the elixir that binds the organization together, ensuring a seamless transition of leadership.

Wisdom in Consultation: Seeking Counsel from Krishna

Yudhishthira's wisdom is magnified through his penchant for seeking counsel, notably from Krishna. In succession amidst adversity, leaders must recognize the value of wise counsel. Consulting mentors and advisors provides a broader perspective, enhancing the quality of decisions made during critical transitions.

Strategic Vision: Navigating the Chessboard of Succession

Yudhishthira's strategic vision, showcased in his adept moves on the chessboard of the Kurukshetra War, becomes a beacon for leaders in the realm of succession planning. The ability to see beyond immediate challenges and anticipate future moves is a crucial trait for steering organizations through tumultuous transitions.

Transparency in Leadership: Illuminating the Path Ahead

Yudhishthira's transparent leadership style is akin to a lantern that illuminates the path ahead. In succession amidst adversity, leaders are encouraged to be transparent, providing clarity and insight into the decision-making process. Transparency becomes the bedrock for trust, essential for a harmonious transition.

Resilience in the Face of Setbacks: Yudhishthira's Steely Resolve

Yudhishthira's resilience, evident in his ability to rise from setbacks, stands as a testament to his steely resolve. Leaders navigating succession amidst adversity must embody resilience. The capacity to rebound from challenges ensures that the organization weathers the storm and emerges stronger on the other side.

Effective Communication: Yudhishthira's Art of Persuasion

Yudhishthira's prowess in effective communication and persuasion is a leadership tool of immense value. In the context of succession, leaders must master the art of conveying their vision and decisions persuasively. Clear and compelling communication fosters understanding and buy-in from stakeholders.

Adaptability to Change: Embracing the Winds of Transformation

Yudhishthira's adaptability to change, especially during the years of exile, showcases a leadership quality indispensable in times of adversity. Leaders in succession planning must embrace the winds of transformation, recognizing that adaptability ensures not only survival but also evolution in the face of change.

Empathy in Leadership: Yudhishthira's Compassion

Yudhishthira's compassion, particularly towards Karna, highlights the role of empathy in leadership. In succession amidst adversity, leaders are encouraged to empathize with the challenges faced by the transitioning team. A compassionate leader fosters a supportive environment, easing the journey through change.

Jacinda Ardern's Leadership in Crisis

Yudhishthira's leadership qualities during adversity find resonance in Jacinda Ardern, Prime Minister of New Zealand. Yudhishthira's calm demeanour and strategic decision-making during challenges parallel Ardern's leadership during crises, such as the Christchurch Mosque shootings and the COVID-19 pandemic. Ardern's ability to lead with empathy, transparency, and resilience showcases Yudhishthira-like qualities that contribute to a smooth transition amidst adversity.

As we unravel the multifaceted leadership tapestry of Yudhishthira, the echoes of his virtues resonate through the corridors of time. His qualities, homed in the crucible of adversity, serve as a compass for modern leaders charting the course of succession planning. Yudhishthira's symphony of leadership, composed of dharma, composure, inclusivity, and strategic vision, becomes a timeless melody that reverberates through the annals of leadership literature.

In the grand theatre of succession amidst adversity, leaders are urged to draw inspiration from Yudhishthira's playbook. Each leadership trait is a note in the orchestration of a seamless transition, a crescendo that transforms challenges into opportunities for growth and transformation. As leaders navigate the tempests of succession, may they heed the timeless wisdom of Yudhishthira, forging a path that not only endures the trials of adversity but emerges triumphant on the other side.

CHAPTER SIX

Mentorship and Guidance: Krishna's Wisdom

Nurturing Success: Unveiling the Art of Mentorship through Krishna's Wisdom

In the grand tapestry of the Mahabharata, the divine discourse between Lord Krishna and Arjuna emerges as a profound beacon of guidance. This exploration delves into the depths of Krishna's wisdom, unravelling his role as a mentor to Arjuna and extracting timeless lessons for the art of mentorship in the context of successful succession. As we traverse the corridors of this sacred conversation, we discover the nuances of mentorship that transcend epochs and resonate with contemporary leaders navigating the intricate path of succession.

The Cosmic Mentorship:

Krishna, the cosmic guide, and charioteer, assumes the role of a mentor par excellence in the Bhagavad Gita. His counsel to Arjuna, poised on the precipice of war and moral dilemma, becomes a metaphor for mentorship that transcends the battlefield of Kurukshetra and extends into the arena of leadership succession. In dissecting Krishna's wisdom, we unearth a treasure trove of insights, shedding light on the principles that underpin successful mentorship.

The Art of Active Listening: Krishna's Attentive Ear

Krishna's ability to actively listen to Arjuna's concerns becomes a cornerstone of effective mentorship. In the context of succession planning, mentors are urged to emulate Krishna's attentive ear, fostering an environment where protégés feel heard and understood. The art of active listening lays the foundation for meaningful mentor-mentee relationships.

Strategic Questioning: Probing the Depths of Understanding

Krishna's strategic questioning of Arjuna's beliefs and convictions serves as a potent tool in mentorship. Mentors engaged in succession planning should adopt the art of strategic questioning, probing the depths of understanding to unearth hidden insights and challenge mentees to reflect on their assumptions and decisions.

Clarity in Guidance: Krishna's Illuminating Discourse

Krishna's clear and illuminating discourse in the Bhagavad Gita provides a model for mentors to follow. In the realm of succession planning, mentors are encouraged to provide clarity in their guidance. Clear communication becomes the torchlight that guides mentees through the complex labyrinth of leadership transitions.

Emotional Intelligence: Krishna's Compassion and Understanding

Krishna's compassion and understanding towards Arjuna's emotional turmoil exemplify emotional intelligence in mentorship. In the context of succession, mentors must cultivate emotional intelligence, recognizing and empathizing with the emotional challenges that accompany leadership transitions.

Balancing Support and Challenge: Krishna's Nuanced Approach

Krishna's nuanced approach of providing both support and challenge to Arjuna underscores the delicate balance mentors must strike. In succession planning, mentors should aim to support mentees in their growth while also challenging them to stretch beyond their comfort zones, fostering a robust developmental journey.

Encouraging Self-Reflection: Krishna's Call to Inner Inquiry

Krishna's encouragement for Arjuna to engage in self-reflection becomes a guiding principle for mentors. Mentors in succession planning should inspire mentees to embark on a journey of inner inquiry, fostering self-awareness and a deeper understanding of their leadership capabilities and aspirations.

The Role of Trust: Arjuna's Unwavering Trust in Krishna

Arjuna's unwavering trust in Krishna illustrates the pivotal role of trust in mentorship. Mentors must cultivate a foundation of trust with their mentees, creating a safe space for open dialogue, vulnerability, and the sharing of challenges and aspirations related to succession.

Cultivating Resilience: Arjuna's Transformation through Adversity

Arjuna's transformation from despondency to resilience under Krishna's guidance imparts a crucial mentorship lesson. Mentors engaged in succession planning should focus on cultivating mentees' resilience, helping them navigate adversity and emerge stronger through the challenges inherent in leadership transitions.

Holistic Development: Krishna's Guidance Beyond the Battlefield

Krishna's guidance extends beyond the immediate battlefield concerns, encompassing broader life principles. In mentorship for succession planning, mentors are encouraged to adopt a holistic approach, considering not only the professional but also the personal and ethical dimensions of leadership development.

Empowering Decision-Making: Krishna's Call for Self-Empowerment

Krishna's emphasis on Arjuna's duty and the power within him becomes a clarion call for mentors to empower mentees in their decision-making. In the realm of succession, mentors should instil a sense of self-empowerment, enabling mentees to take ownership of their leadership journey.

Warren Buffett and Charlie Munger's Partnership

Krishna's guidance to Arjuna serves as a metaphor for mentorship in successful succession. Warren Buffett and Charlie Munger's partnership at Berkshire Hathaway embodies this wisdom. Much like Krishna guiding Arjuna through the complexities of war, Buffett's mentorship has been pivotal in Munger's understanding and decision-making. Their enduring partnership highlights the importance of mentorship in navigating successions successfully.

As we navigate the celestial wisdom embedded in Krishna's mentorship of Arjuna, the echoes of timeless guidance reverberate through the realms of leadership and succession planning. The art of mentorship, as unveiled in the cosmic discourse of the Bhagavad Gita, becomes a sacred thread connecting the ancient with the contemporary.

Leaders engaged in succession planning are beckoned to draw inspiration from Krishna's wisdom, embracing the role of mentorship as a transformative force. The principles of active listening, strategic questioning, emotional intelligence, and trust-building, woven into Krishna's mentorship, provide a blueprint for mentors seeking to guide their protégés through the intricate dance of succession. In the cosmic ballet of leadership, may mentors and mentees alike find resonance with Krishna's timeless teachings, fostering an enlightened path toward seamless succession and enduring leadership legacies.

CHAPTER SEVEN

Navigating Family Dynamics: Lessons from Sita and Kaikeyi

The Intricacies of Family Dynamics: Unravelling Lessons from Sita and Kaikeyi in Succession

In the vast tapestry of ancient epics, the Ramayana stands as a profound exploration of familial dynamics, where the experiences of Sita and Kaikeyi offer invaluable lessons for those navigating the complexities of succession. This exploration delves into the intricate threads of family relationships woven into the narratives, drawing parallels from the challenges faced by Sita and Kaikeyi. As we embark on this journey through the Ramayana, we unravel the timeless lessons that emerge from the trials of managing familial complexities during succession.

The Domestic Odyssey:

Sita, revered as the epitome of virtue and devotion, and Kaikeyi, entangled in the complexities of ambition and familial expectations, present contrasting portraits in the domestic odyssey of the Ramayana. Their stories become mirrors reflecting the intricacies of family dynamics, offering profound insights for contemporary leaders engaged in succession planning amidst familial complexities.

Balancing Personal Aspirations: Sita's Sacrifice and Kaikeyi's Ambition

Sita's selfless sacrifice during her exile and Kaikeyi's ambition for Bharata's ascension illuminate the delicate balance between personal aspirations and familial responsibilities. In the context of succession, leaders are urged to navigate this balance, ensuring that individual ambitions do not compromise the harmony and unity within the family or organization.

Communication and Trust: The Strained Bonds of Ayodhya

The strained bonds between Rama, Sita, and the people of Ayodhya following Sita's exile and Kaikeyi's role in it underscore the importance of communication and trust in familial and organizational settings. In succession planning, leaders must prioritize open and transparent communication to build and maintain trust within the family and the wider organizational structure.

The Role of Influencers: Manthara's Poisonous Counsel and Family Dynamics

Manthara's poisonous counsel, leading Kaikeyi down a destructive path, emphasizes the influence of external factors on family dynamics. Leaders engaged in succession planning should be aware of potential influencers and their impact on familial relationships, guarding against toxic counsel that could disrupt the smooth transition of leadership.

Loyalty and Allegiance: Sita's Unwavering Devotion and Kaikeyi's Dilemma

Sita's unwavering devotion to Rama and Kaikeyi's internal dilemma between maternal love and political aspirations shed light on the complexities of loyalty and allegiance within families. In succession planning, leaders are encouraged to foster an environment where loyalty is balanced with critical thinking, ensuring that family members remain aligned with the organization's values.

The Impact of Exile: Sita's Resilience and Kaikeyi's Reflection

Sita's resilience during exile and Kaikeyi's subsequent reflection on her choices illuminate the transformative potential of adversity. Leaders navigating succession amidst family dynamics should recognize the impact of change and provide support to family members undergoing transitions, fostering resilience and facilitating positive transformations.

Cultural and Traditional Influences: Sita's Virtue and Kaikeyi's Divergence

Sita's embodiment of virtue and adherence to cultural norms contrast with Kaikeyi's divergence from traditional expectations. In succession planning, leaders must be cognizant of cultural and traditional influences within the family, ensuring that transitions respect and align with these values to maintain familial harmony.

The Consequences of Decisions: Sita's Purity and Kaikeyi's Isolation

The consequences of Sita's unwavering purity and Kaikeyi's decisions leading to her own isolation underscore the far-reaching effects of familial choices. Leaders in succession planning should carefully weigh the potential outcomes of decisions, considering the long-term impact on family dynamics and relationships.

The Role of Patience: Sita's Endurance and Kaikeyi's Haste

Sita's endurance during exile and Kaikeyi's hasty decisions highlights the contrasting roles of patience in family dynamics. Leaders engaged in succession planning should exercise patience, allowing family members the time needed to adapt and ensuring that decisions are made with thoughtful consideration.

Emotional Intelligence in Leadership: Understanding Sita's Heart and Kaikeyi's Motivations

Sita's emotional intelligence, reflected in her understanding of Rama's heart, stands in contrast to Kaikeyi's motivations driven by personal desires. In succession planning, leaders should prioritize emotional intelligence, recognizing and empathizing with the emotions and motivations of family members to foster a cohesive transition process.

Reconciliation and Healing: Sita's Return and Kaikeyi's Redemption

Sita's return and Kaikeyi's eventual redemption signify the potential for reconciliation and healing within families. Leaders in succession planning should actively work towards reconciliation, creating opportunities for healing and rebuilding familial relationships that may have been strained during the transition process.

Walmart's Family Dynamics and Succession

Drawing parallels from Sita and Kaikeyi's challenges, Walmart's family dynamics and succession planning provide insights. The Walton family, akin to a familial structure, has navigated generational shifts in leadership. The challenges faced by Walmart's heirs and their ability to manage family complexities during succession showcase the importance of addressing familial dynamics in organizational leadership transitions.

As we navigate the tales of Sita and Kaikeyi within the Ramayana, the echoes of their experiences reverberate through the corridors of familial and organizational leadership. The lessons drawn from these stories become guideposts for contemporary leaders engaged in the intricate dance of succession amidst familial complexities.

In the delicate balance of personal aspirations and familial responsibilities, communication and trust become the mortar that binds families together. The impact of external influences, the transformative potential of adversity, and the role of cultural and traditional influences must be carefully considered. Leaders must recognize the consequences of decisions, exercise patience, and prioritize emotional intelligence to navigate family dynamics successfully during succession.

The domestic odyssey of Sita and Kaikeyi becomes a timeless narrative, offering profound insights for leaders seeking to harmonize familial complexities during transitions. In the symphony of succession planning, may leaders draw inspiration from these ancient tales, weaving a tapestry of familial relationships that endures the tests of time and ensures a legacy of unity and prosperity for generations to come.

CHAPTER EIGHT

Effective Communication: Bhishma Pitamah's Strategies

Artful Discourse: Decoding Bhishma Pitamah's Strategies in Effective Succession Communication

In the grand tapestry of the Mahabharata, the character of Bhishma Pitamah stands as a beacon of wisdom and experience. This exploration delves into the nuances of Bhishma's communication strategies, unravelling the artful discourse he employed to convey crucial information related to succession. As we navigate the labyrinth of his strategies, we draw parallels to contemporary leadership challenges, seeking timeless lessons for effective communication in the delicate context of succession planning.

The Communicative Odyssey:

Bhishma Pitamah, the venerable patriarch of the Kuru dynasty, faced intricate challenges in communicating vital succession-related information during the tumultuous events of the Mahabharata. His strategies, a masterful blend of eloquence and prudence, offer a rich reservoir of insights for leaders in the modern era engaged in the complex terrain of succession planning.

Strategic Timing: Bhishma's Patience and Astuteness

Bhishma's mastery in choosing the right moment for communication is akin to a seasoned chess player contemplating moves. In succession planning, leaders must embody patience and astuteness, selecting opportune moments to convey crucial information. Timing, as Bhishma exemplifies, is a strategic element that can profoundly impact the reception of succession-related messages.

Candid Transparency: Bhishma's Unveiling of Harsh Realities

Bhishma's unflinching transparency, even when conveying harsh realities, showcases the power of Candor in communication. Leaders in succession planning should adopt a transparent approach, openly addressing challenges and potential pitfalls. This honesty establishes a foundation of trust, crucial for navigating the complexities of succession.

Cultural Sensitivity: Bhishma's Adherence to Kshatriya Values

Bhishma's communication is deeply rooted in Kshatriya values, reflecting cultural sensitivity. In contemporary succession planning, leaders should be attuned to the cultural context, ensuring that communication aligns with the values and traditions of the organization. This cultural resonance enhances the authenticity and receptiveness of the message.

Storytelling as a Medium: Bhishma's Narrative Mastery

Bhishma's adept use of storytelling as a medium for communication is a lesson in narrative mastery. Leaders engaged in succession planning can leverage storytelling to convey complex information in a relatable and memorable manner. Stories become vessels that carry the essence of succession-related messages, resonating with the audience on a deeper level.

Emotional Intelligence in Speech: Bhishma's Empathy and Understanding

Bhishma's speech is infused with emotional intelligence, characterized by empathy, and understanding. In succession planning, leaders must be attuned to the emotional nuances of their audience. An empathetic approach, as Bhishma demonstrates, fosters connection and receptivity, facilitating a more effective transmission of critical information.

Adaptability in Expression: Bhishma's Versatility in Communication Styles

Bhishma's versatility in communication styles, adapting to the context and audience, showcases a key leadership trait. Leaders in succession planning should be adaptable in their expression, tailoring communication to suit various stakeholders. Whether addressing family members, advisors, or the wider organization, a flexible communication style enhances resonance and impact.

Clarity in Vision: Bhishma's Articulation of Long-Term Goals

Bhishma's articulation of the long-term vision for Hastinapura serves as a model for leaders in succession planning. Communication should not only address immediate concerns but also articulate a clear vision for the future. Leaders must paint a vivid picture of the organization's trajectory, ensuring that stakeholders comprehend the broader context of succession-related decisions.

Crisis Communication: Bhishma's Calm Amidst Turmoil

Bhishma's ability to maintain composure and articulate messages during moments of crisis is a hallmark of effective crisis communication. Leaders in succession planning should emulate this calm demeanour, providing reassurance and clarity in times of turbulence. A composed leader becomes a stabilizing force, instilling confidence amid uncertainty.

The Art of Diplomacy: Bhishma's Tactful Communication

Bhishma's tactful communication, especially in delicate matters, highlights the art of diplomacy. Leaders navigating succession challenges should employ diplomacy in their communication, especially when addressing sensitive issues. Tactful articulation fosters a harmonious environment, essential for the success of succession plans.

Feedback Loop: Bhishma's Openness to Input and Adjustment

Bhishma's openness to input and adjustment, demonstrated through his interactions with advisors, underscores the importance of a feedback loop. Leaders in succession planning should actively seek input, creating a two-way communication channel. This openness enhances the quality of decision-making and ensures that communication remains a dynamic and evolving process.

Elon Musk's Communication at Tesla

Bhishma's communication strategies in conveying crucial succession-related information find resonance in Elon Musk's leadership at Tesla. Musk's transparent and direct communication about Tesla's plans, challenges, and innovations mirrors Bhishma's effective communication during the Kurukshetra War. Musk's approach exemplifies how clear communication can foster trust and alignment during leadership transitions.

As we traverse the communicative odyssey of Bhishma Pitamah, the tapestry of his strategies unfolds as a timeless guide for leaders in succession planning. The lessons drawn from his artful discourse transcend the ancient battlefield of Kurukshetra, resonating with the challenges faced by modern leaders in steering organizations through the complexities of succession.

Strategic timing, candid transparency, cultural sensitivity, and emotional intelligence emerge as pillars of effective communication in the delicate context of succession planning. Bhishma's legacy becomes a living testament to the enduring power of well-crafted communication, illustrating that the way information is conveyed holds the key to navigating familial and organizational transitions successfully.

In the symphony of leadership, may leaders draw inspiration from Bhishma's strategies, weaving a narrative of succession that resonates with clarity, empathy, and adaptability. As the echoes of his wisdom reverberate through time, may they guide leaders in communicating not only the intricacies of succession but also the enduring vision that propels organizations toward a future of prosperity and longevity.

CHAPTER NINE

Building a Succession Framework: Ravana's Downfall

The Abyss of Ambition: Unravelling Ravana's Downfall as a Cautionary Tale in Building a Succession Framework

In the timeless epic of the Ramayana, the character of Ravana stands as a formidable figure, marked by ambition, power, and, a tragic downfall. This exploration delves into the intricacies of Ravana's reign and his ultimate demise, weaving a cautionary tale about the consequences of lacking a structured succession plan. As we dissect the lessons from Ravana's downfall, we draw parallels to contemporary leadership challenges, seeking insights to build a robust succession framework that guards against the pitfalls that befell the mighty Lanka.

The Throne of Ambition:

Ravana, the formidable king of Lanka, with ten heads symbolizing his immense knowledge and prowess, epitomizes the perilous journey of unbridled ambition. His narrative unfolds as a cautionary tale for leaders, a stark reminder that even the most powerful can crumble when the foundations of succession planning are neglected.

The Perils of Personal Ambition: Ravana's Insatiable Thirst for Power

Ravana's insatiable thirst for power becomes the fulcrum of his downfall. In the context of succession planning, leaders must heed the warning against allowing personal ambition to overshadow the collective welfare. A structured succession plan ensures that the pursuit of individual aspirations does not compromise the stability and continuity of the organization.

The Importance of Governance: Lanka's Unravelling Amidst Chaos

Ravana's governance, marked by chaos and a lack of order, becomes a cautionary example of the importance of effective leadership in building a succession framework. Leaders should recognize that governance extends beyond the present reign, necessitating a structured plan for continuity. A well-crafted succession framework is the cornerstone of sustained governance.

Neglecting Talent Development: Ravana's Shortsighted Leadership

Ravana's shortsightedness in neglecting talent development within his kingdom becomes a pivotal aspect of his downfall. Leaders engaged in succession planning must prioritize talent development, identifying and nurturing potential successors. Neglecting this crucial aspect leaves an organization vulnerable to leadership vacuums and potential chaos.

Disregard for Counsel: Ravana's Hubris and Isolation

Ravana's hubris and isolation, evident in his disregard for wise counsel, echo through the corridors of leadership cautionary tales. In succession planning, leaders must remain open to counsel, fostering a culture of collaboration and informed decision-making. The consequences of isolating oneself from valuable advice can be dire, as exemplified by Ravana's tragic fate.

Legacy Overhaul: Ravana's Failure to Nurture Successors

Ravana's failure to nurture potential successors leads to a legacy overhaul in Lanka. Leaders must recognize that succession planning involves a continuous process of nurturing and grooming successors, ensuring a seamless transition. The inability to pass on leadership responsibilities can result in a radical shift, potentially destabilizing the very foundations of an organization.

Structural Weaknesses: Lanka's Vulnerability in the Absence of Succession Planning

Lanka's vulnerability, exposed in the absence of a structured succession plan, becomes a cautionary lesson for leaders. The structural weaknesses within an organization, if unaddressed, can lead to its downfall. Leaders must fortify these structural pillars through robust succession planning, ensuring resilience and adaptability to changing circumstances.

The Dangers of Nepotism: Ravana's Favouritism and Its Repercussions

Ravana's favouritism, especially toward his son Indrajit, underscores the dangers of nepotism in leadership. Leaders engaged in succession planning should be vigilant against undue favouritism, ensuring that successors are chosen based on merit, capabilities, and alignment with organizational values. Nepotism can compromise the integrity and effectiveness of a succession plan.

Lack of Contingency Planning: Ravana's Unpreparedness for Adversity

Ravana's unpreparedness for adversity, symbolized by his lack of contingency planning, becomes a crucial lesson in succession. Leaders must anticipate and prepare for unforeseen challenges, recognizing that succession planning involves more than the routine passing of the mantle. A well-rounded plan includes contingencies to navigate through turbulent times.

The Cost of Ego: Ravana's Reluctance to Adapt

Ravana's reluctance to adapt, driven by ego, becomes a poignant reminder of the costs associated with inflexibility. Leaders engaged in succession planning must be willing to adapt to changing landscapes, technologies, and paradigms. Ego-driven resistance to change can lead to obsolescence and the downfall of an organization.

Ethical Leadership: Ravana's Moral Bankruptcy and Consequences

Ravana's moral bankruptcy, marked by unethical actions, serves as a cautionary tale for leaders to uphold ethical standards. In succession planning, leaders must prioritize ethical leadership, recognizing that the erosion of ethical principles can lead to internal decay and external condemnation, resulting in downfall.

Lack of Succession Planning in Family Businesses

Ravana's downfall due to the absence of a structured succession plan is mirrored in family businesses that neglect succession planning. Many family-owned enterprises face challenges and disruptions when transitioning to the next generation. The absence of a clear succession framework often leads to internal conflicts, impacting the business's stability, underscoring the cautionary tale from Ravana's downfall.

As we unravel the cautionary tale embedded in Ravana's downfall, the echoes of his mistakes reverberate through the annals of leadership wisdom. The Ramayana becomes a reservoir of insights for contemporary leaders engaged in the delicate task of building a succession framework that withstands the tests of time and adversity.

The perils of personal ambition, the importance of governance, and the dangers of neglecting talent development stand as pillars of leadership wisdom derived from Ravana's tragic narrative. Leaders must diligently address structural weaknesses, resist nepotism, and embrace contingency planning to fortify their organizations against the uncertainties of the future.

In the symphony of leadership, may leaders draw inspiration from Ravana's cautionary tale, using it as a compass to navigate the complexities of succession planning. As the lessons from Lanka's downfall echo through time, may they guide leaders toward a future where structured succession plans stand as bulwarks against the abyss of unbridled ambition, ensuring the enduring prosperity and continuity of their organizations.

Legacy and Heritage: Bharata's Exemplary Rule

Beyond the Crown: Unveiling Bharata's Legacy and Its Influence on Successful Succession

In the grand tapestry of the ancient Indian epic Ramayana, the character of Bharata emerges as a beacon of commitment, responsibility, and unwavering dedication to upholding the family legacy. This exploration delves into Bharata's exemplary rule, investigating the profound impact of his commitment on the successful succession of the Ayodhya kingdom. As we navigate the corridors of Bharata's legacy, we unravel timeless lessons for contemporary leaders engaged in the delicate task of ensuring a seamless transition that preserves and enhances the family or organizational heritage.

The Throne of Responsibility:

Bharata, the second son of King Dasharatha and Queen Kaikeyi, stands as an epitome of loyalty and selflessness. His role becomes particularly significant in the context of successful succession, as he exemplifies the principles of commitment to legacy and the responsible transfer of leadership.

Upholding Family Values: Bharata's Commitment to Dharma

Bharata's commitment to dharma, the righteous path, becomes the cornerstone of his exemplary rule. In contemporary succession planning, leaders are urged to align their actions with the organization's core values, ensuring that the legacy passed on is rooted in principles that withstand the test of time.

The Weight of the Crown: Bharata's Reluctance and Sense of Duty

Bharata's initial reluctance to ascend the throne, driven by his sense of duty and respect for his elder brother Rama, reflects the weight of leadership responsibilities. Leaders engaged in succession planning must carry the mantle with a similar sense of duty, recognizing that the crown symbolizes not only authority but also profound responsibility.

Familial Harmony: Bharata's Bridge-Building with Rama

Bharata's efforts to bridge the gap between himself and Rama showcase the importance of familial harmony in successful succession. Leaders must prioritize fostering positive relationships within the family or organization, recognizing that harmony contributes to a smooth transition and continuity in the legacy.

Empathy in Leadership: Bharata's Understanding of Rama's Sacrifice

Bharata's deep empathy and understanding of Rama's sacrifice exemplify qualities crucial for effective leadership. In succession planning, leaders should cultivate empathy, recognizing the sacrifices made by predecessors and understanding the emotional nuances of the transition process.

Vision for Continuity: Bharata's Commitment to Ayodhya's Prosperity

Bharata's vision for Ayodhya's prosperity extends beyond his personal rule, emphasizing the importance of a long-term perspective in leadership. Leaders engaged in succession planning must articulate a vision that transcends immediate concerns, ensuring the continuity and growth of the family or organization over successive generations.

Community Engagement: Bharata's Connection with the Citizens

Bharata's active engagement with the citizens of Ayodhya showcases the importance of community involvement in leadership. Leaders in succession planning should prioritize building and maintaining strong connections with stakeholders, fostering a sense of community and support that transcends changes in leadership.

Institutionalizing Governance: Bharata's Administrative Prowess

Bharata's administrative prowess in institutionalizing governance becomes a model for leaders in succession planning. The establishment of effective governance structures ensures a smooth transition and sets the stage for sustainable success beyond individual leadership tenures.

Balancing Tradition and Innovation: Bharata's Forward-Thinking Approach

Bharata's forward-thinking approach, marked by a balance between tradition and innovation, becomes a lesson for leaders navigating succession. The ability to preserve the core values and traditions while embracing innovation ensures that the legacy remains relevant and adaptable to changing times.

Educational Initiatives: Bharata's Emphasis on Learning and Development

Bharata's emphasis on learning and development, as reflected in his support for educational initiatives, underscores the significance of investing in human capital. Leaders in succession planning should prioritize educational programs, ensuring the continuous development of individuals who will carry the torch forward.

Environmental Stewardship: Bharata's Commitment to Nature

Bharata's commitment to environmental stewardship, demonstrated by his care for nature during Rama's exile, highlights the broader responsibility leaders have toward sustainability. In succession planning, leaders must consider the impact of their decisions on the environment, ensuring a legacy that respects and nurtures the natural world.

Ford's Legacy Leadership

Investigating Bharata's commitment to upholding the family legacy finds resonance in Ford's legacy leadership. The Ford family's dedication to the company's heritage, values, and principles has contributed to its enduring legacy in the automotive industry. The commitment to upholding the family legacy, as seen in Bharata's rule, reflects in how Ford's leadership has prioritized continuity and tradition.

As we unravel the pages of Bharata's exemplary rule, the echoes of his commitment to upholding the family legacy resonate through the corridors of leadership wisdom. The Ramayana becomes a timeless guide for contemporary leaders, offering profound insights into the principles that underpin successful succession.

Upholding family values, carrying the weight of leadership with a sense of duty, fostering familial harmony, and balancing tradition with innovation stand as pillars of Bharata's legacy. Leaders engaged in succession planning must draw inspiration from Bharata's commitment, recognizing that the transition of leadership is not merely a transfer of power but a sacred responsibility to preserve and enhance the legacy for generations to come.

In the symphony of leadership, may leaders emulate Bharata's virtues, weaving a legacy that stands as a testament to their commitment, empathy, and vision. As the baton passes from one generation to the next, may it carry not only the authority of leadership but also the enduring values that define a legacy worth cherishing and preserving.

CHAPTER ELEVEN

Adaptability and Change Management: Pandavas in Exile

Navigating the Wilderness: Unravelling the Pandavas' Adaptive Journey in Exile and Its Relevance to Change Management in Succession

In the epic Mahabharata, the tale of the Pandavas in exile serves as a profound narrative of resilience, adaptability, and the ability to navigate adversities. This exploration delves into the Pandavas' journey during their years in exile, assessing their adaptability and drawing parallels to the dynamic landscape of change management in succession planning. As we embark on this odyssey, we unravel timeless lessons for contemporary leaders, emphasizing the importance of adaptability in steering organizations through the unpredictable terrains of succession transitions.

The Wilderness of Exile:

The Pandavas, exiled from their kingdom due to a game of dice, embarked on a journey that tested their mettle and adaptability. The challenges they faced during exile become a metaphor for the uncertainties and changes that organizations encounter in the complex process of succession planning.

The Unexpected Twist: Pandavas' Response to Exile

The sudden and unexpected twist in the Pandavas' journey, akin to an unforeseen change in leadership, prompts an immediate response. Leaders in succession planning must emulate the Pandavas' resilience, acknowledging that unexpected shifts require swift and strategic responses to maintain stability.

Adapting to New Realities: Pandavas' Transformation in Exile

The Pandavas' transformation during exile, marked by the acquisition of new skills and alliances, exemplifies the adaptability required in the face of change. Leaders navigating succession planning should be open to acquiring new perspectives, skills, and relationships to effectively lead their organizations through periods of transition.

The Importance of Unity: Pandavas' Cohesion in Diversity

The Pandavas' unity amidst diversity becomes a pivotal lesson for leaders engaged in succession planning. The ability to foster cohesion among diverse talents and perspectives ensures a harmonious transition. Just as the Pandavas remained united, leaders must forge a collaborative spirit within the organization.

Strategic Alliances: Pandavas' Collaborations in Exile

The Pandavas' strategic alliances during exile underscore the importance of collaboration in navigating change. Leaders in succession planning should actively seek and cultivate alliances, both internal and external, to bolster their organizations during transitions and turbulent times.

Resourcefulness in Scarcity: Pandavas' Ingenious Solutions

The Pandavas' resourcefulness in the face of scarcity during exile provides a lesson in innovative problem-solving. Leaders must develop the ability to find ingenious solutions to challenges that arise during succession transitions, ensuring the organization thrives even in resource-constrained environments.

Leadership in Diversity: Yudhishthira's Inclusive Approach

Yudhishthira's inclusive leadership style, evident in his ability to accommodate diverse perspectives within the Pandavas, becomes a model for leaders in succession planning. Embracing diversity in thought and background fosters a rich environment for decision-making and problem-solving during transitions.

Crisis Management: Pandavas' Response to Challenging Situations

The Pandavas' response to challenging situations during exile becomes a case study in crisis management. Leaders in succession planning should develop robust crisis management strategies, anticipating and effectively responding to unforeseen circumstances that may arise during the transition process.

Learning from Adversity: Pandavas' Transformative Experiences

The Pandavas' transformative experiences during exile emphasize the value of learning from adversity. Leaders should view challenges as opportunities for growth, using the lessons gained during succession planning to enhance their leadership capabilities and the resilience of the organization.

Flexibility in Decision-Making: Pandavas' Pragmatism

The Pandavas' pragmatic decision-making, marked by flexibility, becomes a key attribute for leaders navigating succession. Rigidity in decision-making can hinder the adaptability required for successful transitions. Leaders must remain flexible, adjusting their strategies based on evolving circumstances.

Navigating Political Intrigues: Pandavas' Resilience in the Kamakya Forest

The Pandavas' resilience in the face of political intrigues during their stay in the Kamakya Forest becomes a lesson in navigating organizational complexities. Leaders in succession planning should anticipate and adeptly navigate political dynamics, ensuring a smooth transition in the midst of competing interests.

Leadership Transition: Yudhishthira's Handover to Arjuna

Yudhishthira's handover of leadership responsibilities to Arjuna signifies the importance of a well-planned leadership transition. Leaders in succession planning should prioritize a seamless handover process, ensuring that successors are adequately prepared and equipped to lead the organization.

Return from Exile: Pandavas' Triumph and Lessons for Leaders

The Pandavas' triumphant return from exile symbolizes the successful navigation of change. Leaders engaged in succession planning should draw inspiration from this victory, recognizing that with adaptability, strategic planning, and resilience, organizations can emerge stronger from periods of transition.

Netflix's Transition to Streaming

Assessing the Pandavas' adaptability during exile finds a parallel in Netflix's transition from DVD rentals to streaming. Much like the Pandavas' ability to adapt to diverse environments, Netflix's proactive shift to streaming showcased adaptability and change management. The company's success in navigating this transition reflects the relevance of adaptability in contemporary succession planning.

As we traverse the wilderness of the Pandavas' exile, the lessons learned become a guiding compass for contemporary leaders engaged in the intricate dance of succession planning. The Mahabharata serves as a reservoir of insights, emphasizing the importance of adaptability, unity, resourcefulness, and strategic alliances in the face of change.

The unexpected twists, the transformative experiences, and the triumph over adversity underscore the resilience required in leadership during periods of transition. In the symphony of succession planning, may leaders draw inspiration from the Pandavas' journey, weaving a narrative of adaptability and resilience that ensures the enduring success and continuity of their organizations. Just as the Pandavas emerged stronger from their exile, may organizations thrive amidst change, guided by the timeless lessons embedded in this epic tale.

CHAPTER TWELVE

Conflict Resolution: Dice Game Insights

Navigating the Dice Game: Drawing Insights from the Mahabharata for Conflict Resolution in Family Succession

The Mahabharata, an epic narrative that encapsulates the essence of human dilemmas and conflicts, presents a poignant case study in the form of the infamous dice game. This exploration delves into the intricacies of the dice game, unravelling profound insights for conflict resolution within a family context during succession planning. As we navigate the dynamics of this pivotal event, we extract timeless lessons for contemporary leaders, emphasizing the significance of diplomatic finesse and strategic conflict resolution in ensuring a harmonious transition of power.

The Loaded Dice of Conflict:

The dice game in the Mahabharata serves as a metaphorical arena where familial discord, power struggles, and ethical quandaries converge. The complexities of this narrative provide a fertile ground for gleaning insights into conflict resolution strategies applicable to the challenges of succession planning.

The Game of Power: Symbolism in the Dice Game

The symbolism inherent in the dice game represents the high-stakes nature of power struggles within a family during succession. Leaders engaged in succession planning must recognize the gravity of familial conflicts, understanding that the repercussions can reverberate through generations.

Decoding Intentions: Insights into Shakuni's Machinations

The manipulations orchestrated by Shakuni in the dice game offer insights into deciphering hidden intentions within a family dynamic. Leaders must cultivate an acute awareness of potential manipulations during succession, ensuring a proactive approach to address underlying conflicts before they escalate.

Communication Breakdown: The Pandavas' Failure to Articulate Concerns

The communication breakdown between the Pandavas and the Kauravas, leading to the disastrous dice game, highlights the consequences of ineffective communication in family conflicts. Leaders in succession planning should prioritize open and transparent communication channels to address concerns, fostering a collaborative environment.

Diplomacy Amidst Discord: Krishna's Attempt at Conflict Resolution

Krishna's diplomatic intervention during the dice game serves as a beacon of hope for leaders navigating familial conflicts. The art of diplomacy, as demonstrated by Krishna, becomes a crucial tool for leaders in succession planning to mediate disputes and pave the way for constructive resolutions.

Erosion of Trust: Implications for Family Dynamics

The erosion of trust between the Pandavas and the Kauravas during the dice game underscores the fragility of familial bonds in the face of unresolved conflicts. Leaders must prioritize trust-building measures during succession planning, recognizing that trust forms the bedrock of harmonious familial relationships.

Legal Implications: Dharmic Dilemmas and Ethical Quandaries

The Dharmic dilemmas faced by Yudhishthira during the dice game raise ethical questions that resonate in contemporary succession planning. Leaders must navigate legal and ethical considerations delicately, ensuring that decisions align with principles that uphold the integrity of the family and the organization.

Escalation of Conflict: Draupadi's Humiliation and Its Aftermath

Draupadi's humiliation during the dice game triggers an escalation of conflict with far-reaching consequences. Leaders in succession planning should be vigilant to potential triggers that may escalate conflicts, adopting proactive measures to address grievances and prevent the spiralling of familial discord.

Intervention Strategies: Bhishma's Silence and Lessons for Leaders

Bhishma's silence during the dice game prompts reflection on the consequences of passive bystanders in familial conflicts. Leaders engaged in succession planning must be proactive in addressing conflicts, recognizing the importance of timely intervention to maintain familial harmony.

Forging Alliances: The Pandavas' Quest for Support

The Pandavas' quest for support during the dice game highlights the importance of forging alliances to counter familial conflicts. Leaders in succession planning should actively seek allies within the family and beyond, fostering a support network that contributes to conflict resolution and the overall success of the transition.

Mediation and Arbitration: Seeking Equitable Resolutions

The need for mediation and arbitration, exemplified in the aftermath of the dice game, becomes a valuable lesson for leaders. Establishing fair and impartial mechanisms for conflict resolution ensures that disputes are addressed in a just manner, fostering an environment conducive to successful succession.

Reconciliation Efforts: The Pandavas' Willingness to Rebuild

The Pandavas' willingness to reconcile with the Kauravas after the dice game underscores the importance of reconciliation efforts in familial conflicts. Leaders in succession planning should prioritize rebuilding relationships, recognizing that a willingness to forgive and reconcile contributes to a healthier family dynamic.

Learning from Consequences: Leaders' Responsibility for Future Harmony

The consequences of the dice game serve as a stark reminder of the lasting impact of familial conflicts. Leaders in succession planning bear the responsibility of learning from historical conflicts, ensuring that their actions contribute to future harmony and the sustained success of the family and organization.

Unilever's Unification Decision

Drawing insights from the dice game in Mahabharata, Unilever's unification decision serves as a contemporary case study for handling conflicts within a family during succession. Just as the dice game triggered conflicts among the Pandavas, Unilever's dual-headed structure led to disagreements. The decision to unify its headquarters in London demonstrates effective conflict resolution strategies for organizational harmony during succession.

As we unravel the intricacies of the dice game in the Mahabharata, the echoes of familial conflicts reverberate through the corridors of leadership wisdom. The lessons drawn from this poignant episode become a guiding light for contemporary leaders engaged in the delicate dance of succession planning within family contexts.

Decoding intentions, fostering open communication, diplomatic finesse, trust-building measures, and proactive conflict resolution strategies emerge as pillars of wisdom derived from the dice game. Leaders must navigate the loaded dice of familial conflicts with strategic acumen, recognizing that the ability to address and resolve disputes is instrumental in ensuring a harmonious transition of power.

In the symphony of succession planning, may leaders draw inspiration from the insights gleaned from the Mahabharata, weaving a narrative of conflict resolution that fosters familial harmony and contributes to the enduring success of their organizations. As the dice roll in the intricate game of succession, may the lessons learned guide leaders in making decisions that resonate with fairness, ethics, and the preservation of familial bonds.

CHAPTER THIRTEEN

Leadership Transition: Sugriva's Triumph

Beyond the Jungle Throne: Analysing Sugriva's Triumph in Leadership Transition and Its Implications for Modern Succession Planning

In the timeless epic of the Ramayana, the character of Sugriva emerges as a symbol of triumph and successful leadership transition. His ascent to the throne of the Kishkindha Kingdom, following a turbulent period of exile and power struggles, provides valuable insights for contemporary leaders engaged in the intricate dance of succession planning. As we delve into Sugriva's journey, we unravel timeless lessons and draw parallels to the challenges and opportunities faced by leaders in navigating successful leadership transitions in the modern corporate landscape.

The Jungle Throne of Kishkindha:

Sugriva's triumph in leadership transition unfolds against the backdrop of the lush and challenging landscape of Kishkindha. The lessons derived from his journey are a testament to the resilience, strategic thinking, and adaptability required for effective leadership transitions.

Banished Leadership: Sugriva's Exile and Reflection

Sugriva's exile and time spent in introspection become a metaphor for leaders navigating transitions. Contemporary leaders should recognize the value of reflection during periods of exile or transition, fostering self-awareness and a deeper understanding of their leadership capabilities.

The Importance of Alliance: Sugriva's Partnership with Hanuman

Sugriva's alliance with Hanuman highlights the significance of strategic partnerships in leadership transitions. Leaders engaged in succession planning should actively seek and cultivate alliances, both internal and external, to navigate challenges and enhance the effectiveness of the transition process.

Overcoming Internal Strife: Sugriva's Reconciliation with Vali

Sugriva's reconciliation with Vali exemplifies the importance of resolving internal strife during leadership transitions. Leaders must prioritize healing internal divisions, fostering unity, and ensuring that the transition is not marred by lingering conflicts that could undermine the organization's stability.

Strategic Decision-Making: Sugriva's Plan to Reclaim the Throne

Sugriva's strategic decision-making, particularly his plan to reclaim the throne from Vali, becomes a valuable lesson for leaders in succession planning. Effective decision-making, grounded in a thorough understanding of the organization's dynamics, is crucial for a successful leadership transition.

Adaptability and Flexibility: Sugriva's Response to Changing Circumstances

Sugriva's adaptability to changing circumstances, such as forming an alliance with Rama, underscores the importance of flexibility in leadership transitions. Leaders must be agile in responding to unexpected challenges, adapting their strategies to ensure a smooth transition process.

Effective Communication: Sugriva's Appeal to Rama

Sugriva's appeal to Rama for assistance highlights the importance of effective communication in leadership transitions. Leaders should articulate their vision, challenges, and aspirations clearly to key stakeholders, building trust and garnering support for a successful transition.

Empowering Others: Sugriva's Trust in Hanuman

Sugriva's trust in Hanuman and empowerment of key team members exemplify the importance of delegating responsibilities during leadership transitions. Leaders must identify and empower individuals who can play pivotal roles in ensuring the organization's continuity and success.

Resilience in the Face of Setbacks: Sugriva's Perseverance

Sugriva's perseverance in the face of setbacks, including initial failed attempts to defeat Vali, becomes a lesson in resilience for leaders. Leadership transitions often entail challenges, and leaders must exhibit resilience to overcome obstacles and steer the organization toward success.

Strategic Vision: Sugriva's Rule and the Prosperity of Kishkindha

Sugriva's rule and the subsequent prosperity of Kishkindha underscore the importance of a leader's strategic vision for the organization's future. Leaders engaged in succession planning should articulate a clear vision that guides the organization through the transition and sets the stage for sustained success.

Inclusive Leadership: Sugriva's Embrace of Diversity

Sugriva's inclusive leadership, embracing diverse allies and supporters, becomes a model for leaders in contemporary succession planning. Fostering inclusivity ensures that the transition process is characterized by collaboration, diversity of thought, and a collective commitment to the organization's success.

Ethical Leadership: Sugriva's Commitment to Dharma

Sugriva's commitment to dharma (righteousness) in his leadership aligns with the importance of ethical leadership in succession planning. Leaders must uphold ethical principles, ensuring that the transition is conducted with integrity and in alignment with the organization's values.

Learning from Experience: Sugriva's Growth as a Leader

Sugriva's growth as a leader through his experiences becomes a valuable lesson for leaders in succession planning. Leaders should approach transitions as opportunities for personal and professional development, using the experience to refine their leadership capabilities.

Nurturing Successors: Sugriva's Legacy in Hanuman

Sugriva's legacy, particularly in Hanuman's continued leadership, emphasizes the importance of nurturing successors. Leaders engaged in succession planning should invest in the development of potential successors, ensuring a seamless transfer of leadership and the organization's continued success.

To illustrate the enduring relevance of Sugriva's triumph in modern leadership transitions, we can draw inspiration from successful corporate leadership transitions:

Apple Inc.: Tim Cook's Transition

Tim Cook's successful transition as the CEO of Apple Inc. after Steve Jobs exemplifies strategic decision-making, adaptability to changing circumstances, and a commitment to the organization's vision. Cook effectively communicated his plans, empowered key team members, and demonstrated resilience, leading Apple to continued success.

Microsoft Corporation: Satya Nadella's Leadership

Satya Nadella's leadership transition at Microsoft showcases inclusive leadership, a commitment to ethical principles, and a strategic vision for the company's future. Nadella's focus on diversity, inclusivity, and cloud-based technologies has contributed to Microsoft's resurgence as a leading technology company.

The Walt Disney Company: Bob Chapek's Succession

Bob Chapek's succession as CEO of The Walt Disney Company reflects a commitment to organizational prosperity. Chapek's strategic vision, inclusive leadership, and emphasis on streaming services demonstrate the adaptability required for success in the rapidly evolving entertainment industry.

Amazon: Andy Jassy's Transition

Andy Jassy's transition as CEO of Amazon highlights effective communication, strategic decision-making, and a commitment to ethical leadership. Jassy, known for his role in the success of Amazon Web Services, embodies adaptability and resilience in navigating the complexities of leading a global tech giant.

As we analyse Sugriva's triumph in leadership transition, the parallels to contemporary succession planning become evident. The Ramayana offers a timeless narrative that resonates with the challenges and opportunities faced by leaders in navigating the intricate path of organizational succession.

Sugriva's journey encapsulates the essence of effective leadership transitions — from strategic decision-making and adaptability to effective communication and empowerment of key team members. Contemporary leaders can draw inspiration from Sugriva's triumph, recognizing that the principles embedded in this epic tale provide valuable guidance for ensuring successful leadership transitions in the dynamic landscape of modern organizations.

In the symphony of succession planning, may leaders emulate Sugriva's resilience, strategic acumen, and commitment to ethical leadership, ensuring a legacy of prosperity and continuity for their organizations. As the jungle thrones of modern corporations

CHAPTER FOURTEEN

Inclusive Leadership: Draupadi's Influence

The Tapestry of Inclusivity: Unveiling Draupadi's Influence on Leadership Dynamics in Succession

In the vast tapestry of the Mahabharata, Draupadi emerges as a multifaceted character whose influence extends beyond the conventional roles assigned to women in ancient epics. This exploration delves into Draupadi's pivotal role in shaping leadership dynamics and advocating for inclusivity during the tumultuous period of succession in the Kuru Kingdom. As we unravel Draupadi's influence, we draw parallels to contemporary leadership, emphasizing the enduring relevance of inclusivity in the intricate dance of succession.

The Palace Halls of Hastinapura:

Draupadi's journey unfolds within the opulent yet politically charged halls of Hastinapura. Her influence becomes a force that not only challenges traditional norms but also contributes to reshaping the narrative of leadership, setting a precedent for inclusivity and diversity.

Draupadi's Unconventional Leadership: Challenging Norms

Draupadi's assertiveness challenges traditional gender norms, serving as a catalyst for a paradigm shift in leadership dynamics. In contemporary succession planning, leaders must recognize the value of diverse perspectives, transcending conventional norms to foster a culture of inclusivity.

Advocacy for Equality: Draupadi's Stand for Justice

Draupadi's stand for justice, particularly during the infamous dice game, symbolizes her advocacy for equality. Leaders in modern succession planning should champion equal opportunities, ensuring that diverse talents are recognized, respected, and provided with avenues for leadership roles.

Catalyst for Change: Draupadi's Influence on Yudhishthira

Draupadi's influence on Yudhishthira becomes a catalyst for change, prompting him to question societal norms and consider inclusivity in leadership. Similarly, contemporary leaders should be open to influence, recognizing that diverse perspectives contribute to robust decision-making and effective succession planning.

Draupadi as an Advisor: The Power of Inclusive Counsel

Draupadi's role as an advisor to the Pandavas underscores the power of inclusive counsel. In succession planning, leaders should surround themselves with a diverse group of advisors, fostering an environment where varied perspectives are considered, leading to more informed and inclusive decision-making.

Inclusive Decision-Making: Draupadi's Impact on Governance

Draupadi's impact on governance highlights the importance of inclusive decision-making in leadership transitions. Leaders engaged in succession planning should actively seek input from a diverse array of stakeholders, ensuring that decisions resonate with the broader spectrum of the organization.

Breaking Stereotypes: Draupadi's Stance on Women's Leadership

Draupadi's stance on women's leadership challenges stereotypes and biases prevalent in her time. Contemporary leaders must similarly challenge stereotypes, creating opportunities for individuals from all backgrounds to contribute to leadership, fostering a culture of inclusivity and breaking down barriers.

The Importance of Diversity: Draupadi's Influence on Bhima and Arjuna

Draupadi's influence on Bhima and Arjuna exemplifies the importance of diversity in leadership dynamics. In succession planning, leaders should actively promote diversity within leadership teams, recognizing that varied perspectives enhance creativity, innovation, and adaptability.

Draupadi's Resilience: A Lesson in Inclusive Leadership

Draupadi's resilience, particularly in the face of adversity and societal expectations, becomes a lesson in inclusive leadership. Leaders must exhibit resilience in promoting inclusivity, recognizing that overcoming resistance and fostering cultural change is a gradual yet essential process.

Promoting Equal Opportunities: Draupadi's Vision for the Kingdom

Draupadi's vision for the kingdom goes beyond personal interests, emphasizing the need for equal opportunities for all. Leaders in contemporary succession planning should prioritize creating an inclusive organizational culture that fosters equal opportunities for leadership roles, irrespective of background or identity.

Draupadi's Support for Karna: A Lesson in Unbiased Leadership

Draupadi's support for Karna, despite societal biases, imparts a lesson in unbiased leadership. Leaders in succession planning should be conscious of biases and work towards eliminating them, ensuring that talent and potential are recognized without prejudice.

Nurturing Leadership Talents: Draupadi's Influence on Nakula and Sahadeva

Draupadi's influence on Nakula and Sahadeva emphasizes the importance of nurturing leadership talents in all members of the organization. Leaders engaged in succession planning should actively support the development of leadership skills across diverse individuals, recognizing that leadership potential exists in various forms.

Illuminating the enduring relevance of Draupadi's influence on inclusivity in modern leadership, we can draw inspiration from some examples:

Accenture: Julie Sweet's Leadership

Julie Sweet's leadership as the CEO of Accenture exemplifies inclusivity. She has actively promoted diversity and inclusion within the company, setting targets for gender balance and prioritizing initiatives that foster an inclusive workplace culture.

Salesforce: Marc Benioff's Advocacy for Equal Pay

Marc Benioff, the CEO of Salesforce, has been a vocal advocate for equal pay and gender equality. Under his leadership, Salesforce has taken proactive measures to address pay disparities and create an inclusive work environment.

IBM: Arvind Krishna's Commitment to Diversity

Arvind Krishna, the Chairman and CEO of IBM, has demonstrated a commitment to diversity and inclusion. IBM's initiatives include promoting diverse talent in leadership roles and fostering an inclusive corporate culture.

Microsoft: Satya Nadella's Focus on Inclusive Leadership

Satya Nadella, the CEO of Microsoft, has emphasized the importance of inclusive leadership. Microsoft's initiatives include promoting diversity in hiring, fostering an inclusive workplace culture, and addressing unconscious biases.

As we navigate Draupadi's influence on leadership dynamics and inclusivity, the parallels to contemporary succession planning become evident. The Mahabharata offers a timeless narrative that resonates with the challenges and opportunities faced by leaders in fostering inclusive leadership.

Draupadi's assertiveness, advocacy for justice, and influence on decision-making processes underscore the transformative power of inclusive leadership. Contemporary leaders can draw inspiration from Draupadi's legacy, recognizing that inclusivity contributes to organizational growth.

Managing Opposition: Vibhishana's Loyalty Shift

Navigating Loyalty Shifts: Vibhishana's Lesson in Managing Opposition During Succession

In the intricate narrative of the Ramayana, Vibhishana's loyalty shift stands as a compelling tale of leadership dynamics during periods of succession. This exploration delves into the complexities of managing opposition, drawing valuable lessons from Vibhishana's pivotal role in the Ramayana. As we dissect the nuances of loyalty shifts, we uncover insights that resonate with contemporary leaders engaged in the delicate dance of succession planning, navigating the challenges posed by opposition within their organizational landscapes.

The Citadel of Lanka:

Vibhishana's loyalty shift unfolds against the backdrop of the majestic city of Lanka, ruled by the formidable Ravana. The lessons derived from this loyalty shift are not only a testament to the dynamics of power but also a reflection of the strategic acumen required in managing opposition during succession transitions.

The Dynamics of Loyalty: Vibhishana's Allegiance to Ravana

Vibhishana's initial allegiance to Ravana sets the stage for understanding the dynamics of loyalty in leadership. Contemporary leaders must recognize that loyalty is multifaceted and subject to change, necessitating a nuanced approach to managing opposition during succession.

Recognition of Unjust Leadership: Vibhishana's Moral Dilemma

Vibhishana's moral dilemma, recognizing the unjust leadership of Ravana, becomes a poignant lesson. Leaders in modern succession planning should be attuned to moral considerations, acknowledging the importance of ethical leadership, and addressing concerns of injustice that may give rise to opposition.

Vibhishana's Courageous Opposition: A Lesson in Principled Stand

Vibhishana's decision to oppose Ravana, driven by principles, offers a lesson in taking a principled stand against leadership that deviates from ethical norms. Leaders in succession planning should be prepared to demonstrate courage in opposing practices that may be detrimental to the organization's well-being.

Seeking Alignment with Values: Vibhishana's Alliance with Rama

Vibhishana's alliance with Rama highlights the significance of seeking alignment with values and principles. Leaders engaged in succession planning should prioritize alliances that align with the organization's core values, fostering a cohesive and value-driven transition.

Open Dialogue: Vibhishana's Consultation with Rama

Vibhishana's open dialogue with Rama serves as a model for leaders navigating opposition. Effective communication and consultation with dissenting voices are critical in managing opposition during succession, ensuring that concerns are addressed, and perspectives considered.

Vibhishana's Strategic Contribution: A Lesson in Positive Opposition

Vibhishana's strategic contribution to Rama's cause exemplifies positive opposition, where dissent is channelled constructively for the greater good. Leaders in succession planning should encourage constructive criticism and opposition, recognizing that diverse perspectives contribute to robust decision-making.

Navigating Familial Dynamics: Vibhishana's Loyalty to Family

Vibhishana's loyalty to family, despite opposing Ravana, introduces the complexity of familial dynamics in managing opposition. Contemporary leaders should navigate opposition within familial contexts delicately, balancing loyalty with the need for ethical leadership and organizational well-being.

Public Perception: Vibhishana's Transition and Public Opinion

Vibhishana's transition and the subsequent public perception offer insights into managing opposition in the public eye. Leaders in modern succession planning should be mindful of public opinion, understanding that effective communication and transparency are crucial in shaping perceptions during transitions.

Overcoming Mistrust: Vibhishana's Integration into Rama's Alliance

Vibhishana's integration into Rama's alliance underscores the importance of overcoming mistrust in managing opposition. Leaders engaged in succession planning should actively work towards building trust with dissenting parties, fostering collaboration for the greater success of the organization.

Vibhishana's Leadership in Lanka: A Model for Transitioned Leadership

Vibhishana's leadership in Lanka after the shift highlights the potential for transitioned leadership to bring positive change. Leaders in succession planning should recognize that managing opposition effectively can pave the way for transformative leadership that benefits the organization.

Corporate Governance: Elon Musk and Tesla's Board Opposition

Elon Musk, the CEO of Tesla, has faced opposition from the board regarding his leadership style and tweets. Musk's ability to navigate opposition within the board while continuing to lead Tesla reflects the challenges and dynamics of managing dissent in contemporary corporate governance.

Political Leadership: Angela Merkel's Opposition Handling

Angela Merkel, during her tenure as the Chancellor of Germany, demonstrated adeptness in handling political opposition. Her ability to navigate diverse political opinions and maintain stability offers valuable lessons for political leaders engaged in succession planning.

CHAPTER SIXTEEN

Ethical Decision-Making: Rama's Exile Principles

The Ethical Odyssey: Rama's Exile Principles and Their Impact on Succession Planning

The Ramayana, an ancient epic, unfolds a narrative rich with moral dilemmas and ethical decisions. Rama's exile, driven by unwavering adherence to ethical principles, serves as a timeless guidepost for leaders navigating succession planning. This exploration delves into the intricacies of Rama's ethical decision-making during exile and the profound implications it holds for contemporary leaders steering the delicate path of succession within organizations.

The Expanse of Ayodhya:

Rama's ethical journey unfolds against the vast expanse of Ayodhya, a kingdom steeped in tradition and governed by the principles of dharma. As we dissect Rama's exile principles, we unveil lessons that resonate with the complexities of ethical decision-making in succession planning, shedding light on the enduring importance of moral fortitude.

Dharma as the Guiding Light: Rama's Commitment to Righteousness

Rama's adherence to dharma becomes the guiding light of his ethical decision-making. Contemporary leaders should recognize the significance of anchoring decisions in a moral compass, ensuring that ethical principles guide every aspect of succession planning.

Sacrifice for the Greater Good: Rama's Personal Sacrifice for Ayodhya

Rama's willingness to sacrifice personal happiness for the greater good of Ayodhya exemplifies a profound ethical choice. Leaders engaged in succession planning should be prepared to make sacrifices that align with the long-term welfare of the organization, prioritizing collective benefit over personal gain.

Leadership by Example: Rama's Influence on Bharata

Rama's ethical conduct serves as a model for leadership by example, influencing Bharata to follow a path of righteousness. Leaders in contemporary succession planning should recognize the impact of their ethical decisions on the behaviour and choices of those involved in the transition.

Transparency and Communication: Rama's Openness with Sita

Rama's transparency and open communication with Sita regarding his decision to go into exile showcase ethical leadership. Leaders in succession planning must prioritize transparent communication, fostering an environment where stakeholders understand the rationale behind decisions and feel engaged in the process.

Navigating Family Dynamics: Rama's Ethical Treatment of Kaikeyi

Rama's ethical treatment of Kaikeyi, despite her role in his exile, illustrates the challenge of navigating family dynamics with integrity. Leaders in succession planning should handle familial complexities with ethical poise, recognizing that ethical treatment of family members is crucial for organizational harmony.

Avoidance of Revenge: Rama's Noble Response to Surpanakha

Rama's noble response to Surpanakha's provocation, avoiding revenge, showcases ethical restraint. Leaders in contemporary succession planning should resist the temptation for retaliatory actions, opting for ethical responses that contribute to a positive organizational culture.

Respect for Natural Resources: Rama's Ethical Stewardship During Exile

Rama's ethical stewardship during exile, including respect for natural resources, imparts a lesson in environmental responsibility. Leaders engaged in succession planning should consider the ethical implications of their decisions on the environment, aligning organizational practices with sustainable principles.

Fair and Impartial Leadership: Rama's Governance in Ayodhya's Absence

Rama's fair and impartial governance in Ayodhya's absence sets a standard for ethical leadership. Leaders in succession planning should prioritize fairness, ensuring that decisions are made impartially and in the best interest of the entire organization.

Rama's Commitment to Vows: Upholding Promises in Leadership

Rama's commitment to his vows during exile underscores the importance of upholding promises in leadership. Leaders in contemporary succession planning should prioritize the fulfilment of commitments, building trust and credibility among stakeholders.

Rama's Humility in Leadership: A Lesson in Ethical Humility

Rama's humility during exile, despite his royal lineage, offers a lesson in ethical leadership. Leaders engaged in succession planning should embody humility, recognizing that ethical decisions are rooted in a deep understanding of one's role and responsibilities.

To elucidate the enduring relevance of Rama's exile principles in modern leadership, we can draw inspiration from

Corporate Social Responsibility: Patagonia's Ethical Stewardship

Patagonia, a renowned outdoor apparel company, exemplifies ethical stewardship by prioritizing environmental sustainability. The company's commitment to reducing its environmental impact and promoting fair labour practices aligns with Rama's ethical approach to natural resources during exile.

Leadership Transparency: Starbucks' Response to Controversies

Starbucks, in response to controversies, has exemplified transparency and accountability. The company's ethical communication and proactive measures to address issues align with Rama's transparent communication during his exile, showcasing the impact of ethical decision-making on organizational reputation.

Employee-Centric Leadership: Salesforce's Commitment to Equality

Salesforce, led by Marc Benioff, has demonstrated ethical leadership by prioritizing equality and inclusivity. The company's commitment to equal pay, diversity, and philanthropy aligns with Rama's emphasis on fairness and impartial governance, showcasing the impact of ethical values on organizational culture.

Environmental Responsibility: Tesla's Pursuit of Sustainable Practices

Tesla, under the leadership of Elon Musk, has been at the forefront of environmentally sustainable practices in the automotive industry. The company's commitment to electric vehicles and renewable energy aligns with Rama's ethical stewardship.

CHAPTER SEVENTEEN

Balancing Tradition and Innovation: Hanuman's Wisdom

The Harmonious Dance: Hanuman's Wisdom in Balancing Tradition and Innovation and Its Relevance to Succession

Within the epic of the Ramayana, Hanuman emerges as a symbol of unwavering devotion and unparalleled wisdom. His ability to balance tradition and innovation while serving Lord Rama provides timeless lessons for leaders navigating succession within contemporary organizations. This exploration delves into the nuances of Hanuman's approach, unravelling insights that resonate with the delicate balance required in successfully managing tradition and innovation during periods of succession.

The Canopy of Lord Rama's Quest:

Hanuman's wisdom unfolds beneath the vast canopy of Lord Rama's quest, an odyssey that blends the sacred traditions of dharma with the dynamic innovation required to overcome formidable challenges. As we scrutinize Hanuman's journey, we draw parallels to the intricacies of succession planning, highlighting the indispensable need to harmonize tradition and innovation for organizational prosperity.

Hanuman's Unyielding Devotion: Tradition as the Foundation

Hanuman's unyielding devotion to Lord Rama serves as the bedrock of tradition. Contemporary leaders engaged in succession planning must recognize the importance of grounding decisions in the organization's core values and traditions, ensuring continuity and cultural integrity.

Loyalty as a Guiding Principle: Hanuman's Traditional Approach

Hanuman's loyalty as a guiding principle reflects a traditional approach to leadership. In succession planning, leaders should prioritize loyalty to the organization's values and heritage, fostering a sense of continuity and stability amid transitions.

Innovation in Service: Hanuman's Ingenious Solutions

Hanuman's ingenious solutions to challenges demonstrate the infusion of innovation in service. Leaders should emulate this approach during succession, encouraging creative problem-solving and adaptability to navigate complexities effectively.

Respecting Authority: Hanuman's Obedience to Lord Rama

Hanuman's obedience to Lord Rama signifies respect for authority, a traditional virtue. Leaders in succession planning should uphold respect for existing structures and hierarchies, fostering stability while embracing innovation where necessary.

Traditional Wisdom: Hanuman's Reliance on Scriptures

Hanuman's reliance on scriptures reflects the importance of traditional wisdom. In succession planning, leaders should draw from the organization's historical knowledge and lessons learned, incorporating traditional insights into contemporary decision-making.

Courageous Adaptation: Hanuman's Leap to Lanka

Hanuman's courageous leap to Lanka showcases the necessity of adapting to new challenges. Leaders in succession planning should exhibit boldness in exploring innovative strategies, even if it means stepping outside traditional comfort zones.

Innovative Problem-Solving: Hanuman's Search for the Sanjivani Herb

Hanuman's search for the Sanjivani herb exemplifies innovative problem-solving. Leaders in succession planning should encourage a culture of continuous improvement and creative problem-solving, infusing innovation into organizational processes.

Adapting to Change: Hanuman's Transformation into a Giant

Hanuman's transformation into a giant to carry the mountain highlights the adaptability required in the face of change. Leaders should foster a mindset that embraces change, integrating innovative practices seamlessly into traditional frameworks during succession.

Respecting Boundaries: Hanuman's Discreet Encounter with Sita

Hanuman's discreet encounter with Sita emphasizes the importance of respecting boundaries. Leaders in succession planning should navigate innovations with sensitivity, ensuring they align with the organization's values and ethics.

Innovation in Collaboration: Hanuman's Alliance with Sugriva

Hanuman's alliance with Sugriva demonstrates innovation in collaboration. Leaders should explore creative partnerships and alliances during succession, fostering synergies that enhance the organization's capabilities.

Traditional Values in Leadership: Hanuman's Humility

Hanuman's humility before Lord Rama embodies traditional values in leadership. During succession, leaders should uphold humility, recognizing the wisdom and experiences of those who have contributed to the organization's legacy.

Apple Inc.: The Legacy of Steve Jobs and Innovative Leadership

Apple Inc., under the visionary leadership of Steve Jobs, exemplifies the harmonious balance between tradition and innovation. While adhering to the core values and design principles established by Jobs, the company continues to innovate with products like the iPhone and MacBook, demonstrating how tradition can coexist with cutting-edge innovation.

Toyota: Kaizen Philosophy and Continuous Improvement

Toyota's success is rooted in its adherence to the traditional Japanese philosophy of Kaizen, emphasizing continuous improvement. While respecting traditional manufacturing principles, Toyota consistently innovates its production processes, showcasing how a commitment to tradition can underpin a culture of ongoing innovation.

Google: Alphabet's Innovative Approach to Diverse Ventures

Google's transformation into Alphabet reflects an innovative approach to diversification. While adhering to the traditional search engine business, Alphabet allows for the exploration of new ventures such as autonomous vehicles and life sciences. This demonstrates how a traditional core can serve as a springboard for innovative exploration during succession.

IBM: The Evolution from Hardware to Cloud Services

IBM's transition from a traditional hardware-focused business to a leader in cloud computing exemplifies strategic innovation. While respecting its legacy in computing hardware, IBM successfully navigated the shift toward cloud services, showcasing how traditional strengths can be leveraged for innovative growth during succession.

In the tapestry of Hanuman's wisdom, leaders engaged in succession planning find a roadmap for navigating the delicate dance between

CHAPTER EIGHTEEN

Crafting Your Succession Epic

Crafting Your Succession Epic: Navigating Leadership Transitions with Wisdom and Foresight

As we embark on the final chapter of our exploration into the intricate world of succession planning, it is time to distil the wealth of knowledge gleaned from the epics of Krishna, Sita, Bhishma, Ravana, Bharata, Pandavas, Dice Game, Sugriva, Draupadi, Vibhishana, Rama, and Hanuman. In this synthesis, we will unravel the essence of successful succession narratives and offer practical guidance inspired by the timeless tales of wisdom, adaptability, and legacy.

The Wisdom of Krishna: Embrace Mentorship and Guidance

In Krishna's role as a wise counsellor, we find the importance of mentorship and guidance in crafting successful succession narratives. Leaders should actively seek mentorship, providing strategic counsel to their teams, fostering a culture of continuous learning and growth. The story of Krishna guiding Arjuna on the battlefield serves as a timeless example of effective mentorship.

Microsoft's Satya Nadella

Satya Nadella's leadership at Microsoft is a contemporary illustration of the impact of wise counsel. He embraced a growth mindset, seeking guidance from mentors and reshaping Microsoft's culture. Under his leadership, the company embraced cloud computing and achieved remarkable success, showcasing the transformative power of mentorship in succession.

Navigating Family Dynamics with Finesse: Insights from Sita and Kaikeyi

The challenges faced by Sita and Kaikeyi shed light on the intricacies of navigating familial complexities during succession. Leaders must approach family dynamics with finesse, addressing conflicts, fostering unity, and prioritizing the well-being of the organizational family. The tale of Sita's exile and Kaikeyi's influence exemplifies the impact of familial decisions on the succession narrative.

Walmart's Succession Planning

Walmart's succession planning provides insights into navigating family dynamics. The Walton family, as major stakeholders, navigated the transition from Sam Walton to subsequent generations. Through careful planning and strategic decisions, they managed to preserve the family legacy while adapting to changing market dynamics.

Prioritize Effective Communication: Bhishma's Strategies for Succession

Bhishma's communication strategies exemplify the significance of effective communication in the context of succession planning. Leaders should articulate their visions, challenges, and decisions clearly, fostering transparency and alignment among stakeholders. Bhishma's pledge of lifelong celibacy and his role in advising the Kuru kings showcase the impact of clear communication on succession.

Alphabet's Leadership Transition

The transition from Larry Page to Sundar Pichai at Alphabet is a testament to effective communication in succession. Page, as Alphabet's CEO, communicated the restructuring plans clearly, and Pichai, who became CEO of both Google and Alphabet, provided transparency about the company's future direction, ensuring a smooth transition.

Implement Structured Succession Plans: Ravana's Downfall as a Cautionary Tale

Ravana's downfall becomes a cautionary tale, emphasizing the consequences of lacking a structured succession plan. Leaders must meticulously design and implement succession frameworks, ensuring a seamless transition and mitigating risks associated with leadership vacuums. Ravana's failure to plan led to chaos and upheaval in his kingdom.

Disney's Succession Planning

Disney's succession planning under CEO Bob Iger exemplifies the importance of structured plans. Iger orchestrated a smooth transition by appointing a successor, Bob Chapek, well in advance. This strategic planning contributed to the continuity of Disney's vision and operations.

Legacy Upheld: Bharata's Commitment to Heritage

Bharata's commitment to upholding family legacy echoes the importance of preserving heritage during succession. Leaders should be devoted to preserving organizational culture, values, and legacy, ensuring continuity and a sense of identity. Bharata's refusal to rule Ayodhya in Rama's absence exemplifies the commitment to heritage.

Ford's Legacy Leadership

Ford's legacy leadership, exemplified by the Ford family's commitment to the company's heritage, is noteworthy. Despite challenges and changing market dynamics, successive generations of the Ford family have maintained a connection to the company's founding principles, contributing to its enduring legacy.

Adaptability and Change Management: Pandavas in Exile

The Pandavas' adaptability during exile becomes a case study for navigating change in succession planning. Leaders should exhibit resilience, flexibility, and a proactive approach to managing uncertainties during transitions. The Pandavas' ability to adapt to diverse environments and challenges showcases the importance of change management.

IBM's Evolution

IBM's evolution from a traditional hardware-focused business to a leader in cloud computing reflects adaptability in succession planning. By embracing new technologies and business models, IBM demonstrated resilience and the ability to navigate change effectively under different leadership eras.

Conflict Resolution: Insights from the Dice Game

The insights drawn from the dice game in Mahabharata serve as a case study for handling conflicts within a family during succession. Leaders should employ effective conflict resolution strategies, fostering harmony and collaboration amid differing viewpoints. The tale of the dice game and the subsequent exile of the Pandavas exemplify the repercussions of unresolved conflicts.

Unilever's Unification Decision

Unilever's conflict resolution and unification decision highlight the importance of resolving conflicts for successful succession. In the face of opposition to its dual-headed structure, Unilever chose to unify its headquarters in London, demonstrating the significance of conflict resolution for organizational harmony.

Leadership Transition Triumph: Sugriva's Lesson

Sugriva's successful leadership transition provides a blueprint for contemporary succession planning. Leaders must analyse, strategize, and execute transitions with a focus on effective communication, adaptability, and empowerment of key team members. Sugriva's leadership triumph after the defeat of Vali serves as a lesson in effective leadership transition.

Apple's Transition from Steve Jobs to Tim Cook

Apple's transition from Steve Jobs to Tim Cook exemplifies a successful leadership transition. Jobs meticulously planned for his succession, and Cook, as the chosen successor, continued Apple's trajectory of innovation. This seamless transition contributed to Apple's sustained success.

Inclusive Leadership: Draupadi's Influence

Draupadi's role in influencing leadership dynamics emphasizes the importance of inclusivity in succession. Leaders should champion diversity, equality, and ethical leadership, recognizing the transformative power of inclusivity in organizational success. Draupadi's stand for justice and her influence on the Pandavas underscore the importance of diversity in leadership.

Johnson & Johnson's Diversity and Inclusion Initiatives

Johnson & Johnson's commitment to diversity and inclusion initiatives reflects Draupadi's influence in contemporary leadership. The company has implemented policies to foster an inclusive workplace, recognizing the value of diverse perspectives in driving innovation and success.

Managing Opposition: Vibhishana's Loyalty Shift as a Lesson

Vibhishana's loyalty shift serves as a lesson in managing opposition during succession. Leaders should navigate opposition with ethical poise, encouraging positive dissent, and building trust with dissenting parties. Vibhishana's decision to shift loyalty to Lord Rama highlights the importance of managing opposition with integrity.

Stone or Stepping Stone: Navigating the Path of Succession

Unveiling the Employee's Role in Succession Planning

In the intricate dance of organizational dynamics, employees play a pivotal role, serving as either steadfast stone anchoring the foundation or stepping stones propelling the organization toward new heights. This chapter delves into the profound concept of "Stone or Stepping Stone" within the context of succession planning. Drawing inspiration from the sagas of Ramayana and Mahabharata, we unravel the importance of identifying the right trajectory for individuals and harnessing their potential for the collective success of the organization.

Hanuman: The Ultimate Stepping Stone in Ramayana:

The character of Hanuman in Ramayana exemplifies the essence of a stepping stone. His unwavering loyalty, resilience, and exceptional capabilities positioned him not merely as a supporting stone but as the catalyst for the triumph of Lord Rama. Hanuman's dedication, proactive mindset, and transformative contributions showcase the potential for an individual to transcend the role of a mere stone, becoming an instrumental force in the success of the mission.

Vidura: The Wise Stone in Mahabharata:

In Mahabharata, Vidura stands out as a symbol of a wise stone in the court of Hastinapura. His sagacious counsel and commitment to righteousness made him an indispensable advisor. Vidura's wisdom and ethical stance positioned him as a foundational stone, providing stability to the kingdom. His role underscores the significance of identifying individuals with inherent qualities that contribute to the organization's resilience and ethical standing.

Identifying Stones and Stepping Stones in the Workplace:

In the contemporary organizational landscape, recognizing employees as either stones or stepping stones is crucial for effective succession planning. Stones may be reliable and consistent but lack the transformative potential to navigate dynamic challenges. Stepping stones, on the other hand, possess the ability to adapt, innovate, and contribute to the organization's evolution.

Nurturing Stepping Stones: Yudhishthira's Leadership Traits:

Yudhishthira's leadership traits in Mahabharata provide insights into nurturing stepping stones within an organization. His ability to recognize and cultivate the strengths of each Pandavas showcases the significance of leadership in transforming individuals into assets for the collective good. Yudhishthira's leadership becomes a blueprint for identifying potential stepping stones and leveraging their capabilities for organizational success.

Avoiding Pitfalls: Duryodhana as the Unyielding Stone:

Duryodhana's character in Mahabharata serves as a cautionary tale of being an unyielding stone in the path of progress. His refusal to acknowledge the potential of the Pandavas, his rigidity, and his inability to adapt led to his downfall. This example underscores the risks associated with ignoring the potential stepping stones within the organization.

Succession Planning Strategies: Recognizing Potential Stepping Stones:

Implementing effective succession planning requires a proactive approach to recognize potential stepping stones among employees. This involves assessing not only current performance but also the ability to adapt, learn, and contribute to the organization's long-term goals. Investing in the development of stepping stones ensures a resilient and dynamic leadership pipeline.

In the journey of organizational success, employees are not mere stones but potential stepping stones, each with the capacity to propel the organization forward. Drawing from the timeless lessons of Ramayana and Mahabharata, we learn that recognizing and nurturing individuals as stepping stones requires keen insight and strategic leadership. As we navigate the complexities of succession planning, may this chapter serve as a guide for leaders to distinguish between stones and stepping stones, fostering a culture of growth, adaptability, and collective triumph.

The Tata Group

In the context of Indian business, the Tata Group stands as an exemplary model of effective succession planning. The conglomerate, founded in 1868, has meticulously crafted a robust system for leadership transition. The Tata Sons, the holding company of the group, ensures a seamless succession process through a combination of meritocracy and family representation.

The Tata Group embraces a comprehensive approach to succession planning, balancing professional competence with family values. The Tata Sons board is constituted by a mix of professionals and family members, ensuring a blend of diverse expertise. The company has a tradition of grooming leaders from within, promoting a culture of continuous learning and development.

An illustrative case is the succession of Ratan Tata by Cyrus Mistry in 2012. Ratan Tata, a respected figure in the business world, had a structured transition plan in place. The selection of Cyrus Mistry was not only based on his family ties but, more importantly, on his capabilities, experience, and alignment with the group's values. However, this transition also highlighted the complexities involved, leading to subsequent changes in leadership.

Infosys

Infosys, one of India's leading IT companies, has set benchmarks in succession planning. Founded in 1981, Infosys has cultivated a culture of grooming leaders from within, emphasizing skill development and leadership readiness.

Infosys has a well-defined leadership institute that focuses on identifying high-potential employees and providing them with tailored development programs. The company encourages a transparent career progression path, ensuring that individuals are aware of the skills and competencies required for higher roles.

The transition from N. R. Narayana Murthy to Nandan Nilekani in the late 2000s is a notable example. The process involved careful planning, mentorship, and a focus on continuity in the company's vision. Nilekani, having been a co-founder, ensured a smooth transition while bringing fresh perspectives to drive the company forward.

Reliance Industries

Reliance Industries, under the leadership of the Ambani family, has been a key player in shaping India's corporate landscape. The company has demonstrated a structured approach to succession planning, with a blend of family legacy and professional competence.

The transition from Dhirubhai Ambani to his sons, Mukesh, and Anil Ambani, showcased a strategic succession plan. The subsequent evolution of leadership within the group has involved a combination of family members and professionals, ensuring a balance between continuity and adaptability.

Mukesh Ambani's strategic leadership and emphasis on innovation have driven the company's growth. The appointment of professionals in key positions, coupled with family representation at the top, reflects a thoughtful approach to succession planning that aligns with the company's dynamic goals.

Aditya Birla Group

The Aditya Birla Group, with interests in sectors ranging from metals to cement, has established itself as a powerhouse in Indian business. The group's approach to succession planning is marked by a blend of familial lineage and professional competency.

The group has a tradition of grooming leaders from within and providing them exposure to diverse business operations. The Birla Leadership Program identifies high-potential executives and hones their skills for leadership roles. The succession planning process is structured, ensuring a smooth transition from one generation to the next.

The transition from Aditya Vikram Birla to Kumar Mangalam Birla exemplifies this approach. Kumar Mangalam Birla, the current chairman, has brought a modern and dynamic outlook to the conglomerate while preserving the family's legacy and values.

HDFC

Housing Development Finance Corporation Limited (HDFC) has been a torchbearer in the financial sector, and its succession planning has been marked by a strategic balance of experience and infusion of fresh leadership.

HDFC's succession planning involves a systematic identification of potential leaders, coupled with a focus on skill development. The company prioritizes talent retention and emphasizes a culture of learning and adaptability.

Aditya Puri's retirement as the CEO in 2020 marked a significant succession event. The appointment of Sashidhar Jagdishan, who had been associated with HDFC for over two decades, exemplifies the company's commitment to grooming internal talent and ensuring a seamless transition.

Wipro

Wipro, a major player in the IT industry, has demonstrated a strategic approach to succession planning by fostering a culture of innovation and leadership development.

Wipro's leadership pipeline is fuelled by various programs that identify and nurture high-potential talent. The company encourages a dynamic and entrepreneurial mindset, preparing leaders for challenges in a rapidly evolving industry.

The transition from Azim Premji to his son, Rishad Premji, showcased a balanced approach to succession. Rishad Premji, with a background in business and technology, brought a fresh perspective while ensuring continuity in Wipro's values. The process involved a careful blend of family representation and professional competence.

These Indian examples illustrate diverse approaches to succession planning, emphasizing the importance of balancing family legacy with professional competence. The success of these transitions lies in careful planning, mentorship, and a commitment to fostering leadership from within the organization. As India's business landscape evolves, these case studies offer valuable insights for organizations aiming to ensure seamless leadership transitions and sustained growth.

Unveiling The Power Of Action

Actions Speak Louder Than Words: Lessons from Mahabharata, Ramayana, and Real-World Leadership

In the grand narratives of Mahabharata and Ramayana, the principle "Actions speak louder than words" resounds through the ages, serving as a timeless guide for leaders navigating the intricate tapestry of responsibilities and ethical dilemmas. In this chapter, we delve into the profound lessons of action-driven leadership, drawing inspiration from the epics and contemporary anecdotes that transcend the pages of ancient scriptures.

Karna's Sacrificial Actions in Mahabharata:

In Mahabharata, the character of Karna stands as an exemplar of actions that define one's character. Karna's unwavering loyalty to Duryodhana and his selfless acts, such as donating his divine armour to Indra in disguise, showcase a commitment that speaks volumes. Karna's actions, driven by principles and sacrifice, reveal the depth of his character, emphasizing that deeds resonate louder than mere words.

Hanuman's Leap of Faith in Ramayana:

Turning our gaze to Ramayana, the tale of Hanuman's devotion and courage unfolds as a testament to action-based leadership. When Hanuman leaps across the ocean to reach Lanka in search of Sita, his actions not only convey his unwavering commitment but also become a defining moment in the narrative. Hanuman's fearless leap demonstrates that actions, especially in the face of adversity, leave an indelible mark and echo louder than mere expressions of intent.

Bhishma's Oath in Mahabharata:

Bhishma Pitamah's solemn oath of celibacy and lifelong dedication to Hastinapura exemplifies the power of actions in shaping destiny. Bhishma's commitment to the throne, despite personal sacrifices, serves as a compelling example of leadership driven by deeds. His actions, deeply rooted in duty, showcase that one's allegiance and sacrifices can shape the course of a kingdom, far beyond the resonance of spoken promises.

Rama's Exile in Ramayana:

The narrative of Lord Rama's voluntary exile in Ramayana reveals profound lessons in leadership through action. Rama's choice to honor his father's word and uphold dharma by embarking on a fourteen-year exile exemplifies decisive and sacrificial leadership. Rama's actions underscore that the true test of leadership lies not just in words but in the choices, one makes, especially when faced with challenging circumstances.

Real-World Leadership: Advocate's Dedication Amidst Recovery:

Transitioning from the epics to a real-world example, consider the story of an advocate who, despite being confined to a hospital bed post-surgery, exhibited a commitment to the organization that transcended personal well-being. While recovering, the advocate ensured that the company's committed work progressed seamlessly. This leader's actions spoke louder than words, showcasing a dedication to the organization's health even when personal health was at stake.

In the world of leadership, Mahabharata and Ramayana offer profound insights into the transformative power of actions. Karna's sacrifice, Hanuman's fearless leap, Bhishma's lifelong commitment, and Rama's voluntary exile stand as timeless examples of how actions resonate through the corridors of history. When juxtaposed with a contemporary tale of an advocate prioritizing organizational health amid personal recovery, the principle "Actions speak louder than words" echoes across epochs, reminding us that true leadership is a manifestation of deeds that transcend mere rhetoric. May these narratives inspire leaders to lead not just with words but with transformative actions that shape legacies and define the very essence of leadership. The main purpose of this book is understanding the tool. Sitting Aside is a powerful tool for a leader to create succession for a sustainable business.